Sweet Dreams of Gingerbread

Sweet Dreams of Gingerbread

Jann Johnson

Sedgewood® Press

New York

For CBS, Inc.
 Editorial Director: *Dina von Zweck*
 Project Coordinator: *Jacqueline Weinbach*

For Sedgewood® Press
 Director: *Elizabeth P. Rice*
 Project Editor: *Lori Labriola*
 Associate Editor: *Leslie Gilbert*
 Production Manager: *Bill Rose*

 Book Designer: *Bentwood Studio/Jos. Trautwein*
 Photography: *Robert Epstein*

ACKNOWLEDGEMENTS

A book always has a supporting cast. In addition to the editors, photographer and book designer I appreciate the talent and help of the following people:
Peter Hempel for his literary input, Gary Johnson, Louis Erickson (Lewis and Neal, Inc.), Neal Brunckhorst (Spice Islands), Tom Burns (American Spice Trade Association), Terry Capuana, Karin Lidbeck, Marsha Brooks-Smith, Carter Berg and Sam Berg.

CREDITS

I gratefully acknowledge the generous loan of products for photography from the following companies:

V.I.P. Fabrics, a division of Cranston Print Works Company for their Christmas story cottons

Thos. K. Woodard, for their lovely antique quilt "Triangle Variation"

Lenox China for their Holiday pattern

C. M. Offray and Sons for yards of glorious ribbon

Laura Ashley for pastel wallpapers and fabrics

Gear Designs for Waechtersbach U.S.A. for a red mug

Gear Designs for Kurt S. Adler for a red patchwork teddy bear

Gear Designs for C. R. Gibson for wrapping paper

American Tree & Wreath Co. for Christmas trees, garlands and wreaths

ISBN: 0-02-496780-7
Library of Congress Catalog Card Number 86-60036
Manufactured in the United States of America.
Distributed by Macmillan Publishing Company, a division of Macmillan, Inc.

10 9 8 7 6 5 4 3 2 1

Contents

Introduction

THE ART OF CREATING decorative gingerbread is a time-honored tradition, usually associated with joyous occasions. The Chinese are said to have developed one of history's earliest cakes: honeyed gingerbread. Some literary references credit a Greek baker who lived around 2800 B.C. as the creator of gingerbread. Recipes improved over time and so did gingerbread's popularity.

Hundreds of years ago, bakers used elaborate wooden molds to shape the cookies into birds, dogs, bears, fish and other shapes. A heart-shaped gingerbread cookie was a romantic gift, which sometimes had an inscription and a small mirror attached. And talk about gilding the lily—at times gingerbread was even embellished with real gold.

In Russia, when Peter the Great was born, more than 100 cakes of gingerbread were part of the celebration; some of the cakes weighed more than 200 pounds. At medieval fairs, stalls selling gingerbread were a familiar sight. Later, Queen Elizabeth I served cookies molded in her guests' likenesses. In Victorian England, street vendors hawked round ginger "snaps" and "buttons."

The fairytale story of Hansel and Gretel's visit to a house made of sweets may have inspired the Germans to build cottages of gingerbread. The custom spread to Colonial America and has remained popular since.

Gingerbread's popularity continues today. The pleasure we have in smelling the spicy scent as the dough bakes is matched by our pleasure in creating decorative forms and shapes. The gingerbread "creations" in this book are designed to inspire you with modern versions of an age-old craft. I hope that every step—from measuring the first spice to placing the last gumdrop—will be a happy one.

General Directions

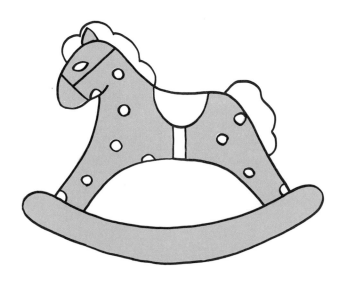

Equipment

This is a general guide to the materials you will need to make splendid gingerbread. Substitutions can be made, and I am sure you will come up with some clever ones.

Measuring Cups and Spoons

All recipes were tested with standard equipment. Usually, dry ingredients are leveled in plastic or metal measuring cups which hold one specific amount, such as ½ cup.

Liquids are usually measured in marked glass cups that also vary in size. Unconventionally, I use a glass 4-cup measure for flour when making the Architectural Dough. It is quite accurate and helpful, since it only has to be refilled once. To test, scoop and level four 1-cup measures of flour into your glass cup to see if it hits the 4-cup line on the nose. When measuring this fool-proof way, interruptions will not cause you to lose count of the flour amount.

Large Mixing Bowls and Custard Cups

The bowls are for cookie dough and icing. The cups are perfect for tinting small amounts of icing.

Electric Mixer

Gingerbread, especially the Architectural Dough, is a rather stiff dough. It can be made by hand or with a portable or standup mixer. I do not recommend a food processor for most doughs, because it works at too high a speed,

and it may not be able to handle a stiff dough. One exception is the Ginger Shortbread recipe; the food processor works well for this particular dough.

Cookie Sheets and Cooling Racks

The flat aluminum kind with one raised edge (a handle of sorts) have been my standbys for years. The bigger, the better.

Large cooling racks are very useful for just-baked cookies. If you do not own a cooling rack, use clean, opened brown paper bags.

Plastic Wrap

Great for wrapping, storing and rolling out dough. Also, cover bowls of icing with plastic wrap. It is a real aid.

Guides or Rulers

The dough's thickness must be kept consistent to ensure correct pattern fit. I find guides essential: accurately cut 2 plastic or wooden strips (approximately $1'' \times 15''$) ¼" or ⅛" thick. They are placed directly on the cookie sheet, on either side of the dough, so that the rolling pin will not sink below their level. In a wink, you will have an accurate thickness. If you don't use strips, measure dough with a ruler.

Rolling Pin

Whether you like the American style with

handles, or the French type without, a long, heavy wooden pin quickly takes care of rolling dough smoothly. Long rolling pins are easiest to use with the above guides, and for rolling out large cookies. Mine is 15″, not including handles.

Long Spatula or Pancake Turner

A long, wide spatula is extremely helpful to loosen large, baked cookies from a baking sheet and to transfer to a cooling rack. A pancake turner and a long knife will do in a pinch.

Patterns and Cookie Cutters

Step-by-step directions for making your own cardboard patterns are given later.

Use plain and fancy cookie cutters for leftovers that can be left plain or glazed. It is great fun to bite into an appealingly-shaped cookie. Somehow it tastes better!

Oven Thermometer and Timer

An accurate timer is essential. All oven temperatures vary, so check yours and adjust baking time accordingly. Always set the timer for a minute or two *less* than the minimum to allow for a too-hot oven. Remember, cookie brownness always has the final say.

Hot Mitts and Kitchen Towel

Use cotton or wool padded mitts to prevent burns. The popular polyester foam mitts do not shield intense heat.

A soft, clean terry kitchen towel works well under cookie sheets to help keep them from slipping when rolling out dough. It is also useful to have when decorating the other side of an iced cookie (Royal Icing only).

Decorating Bags or Cones and Tips

Icing is filled into special plastic or cloth bags fitted with a decorating tip, or a parchment cone that may or may not have a tip. Decorating bags hold a lot of icing, and they are most useful for covering large areas such as bases and the tree centerpiece.

Disposable, easy-to-handle, parchment cones are best for making most projects.

Plain decorating tips, (#3 or its equivalent) are used throughout the book. It produces a line of icing about ³⁄₁₆″. Other tips used are: #1, 2, 4, 12, 14, 190, 225 and 325.

Paste Food Colors and Toothpicks

Paste food colors, which are available by mail in many colors, tint icing in pastels or vibrant colors. Liquid colors tint pastels only and are not really appropriate for this book. Christmas red, lemon yellow, orange, sky blue, leaf green, violet, brown and black are the basics. Toothpicks are used to transfer a bit of color to the icing.

Candy, Drop Flowers and Nuts

For a pleasing effect, aim for different shapes, sizes, colors and textures when you mix candy. Some candy "stains" the icing, leaving a colored ring all around. Red cinnamon candy, jelly beans, gumdrops, candy canes (straight or curved), peppermints, kisses, licorice, raisins, caramels, nuts, silver dragees and multi-colored sprinkles are all good choices. Drop Flowers are made on wax paper using Royal Icing and a #325 tip. (See how-to on page 27.) These are cute and wonderfully ornamental. Small cookies, homemade from canapé cutters or purchased, also work well, and can be decorated before they are used.

Heavy Jars

Three-dimensional projects need to be supported while drying. Straight-sided jars are often better to use than cans, because they do not have rims, and they can fit flush against the cookie. When that's not important (for example;

a cookie roof overhang), cans are perfect, stacked as needed for the correct height.

Cellophane

Clean cellophane is perfect for wrapping large and small cookies. Tie with ribbon for a festive effect that protects while it sparkles!

Bases

Baskets without handles, cutting boards, trays, covered cardboard, styrofoam, or foamcore board, masonite and ¼″ plastic are suitable possibilities. They protect your furniture from direct contact with cookies, as well as provide a foundation for a stylized setting.

Pattern-Making Tools

When making patterns, use any of the following: paper, carbon paper, cardboard, scissors, mat knife, straight edge or ice pick.

Thin paper, such as tissue or tracing paper, is needed to trace designs from the book. If you wish, an 8″ × 10″ sheet of clear plastic placed under the tracing paper will protect the page during tracing. This is a technique used in some design libraries.

Carbon paper, dressmaker's or typist's carbon, is used to transfer designs from paper onto cardboard.

Slick, medium-weight, cardboard such as posterboard found in dimestores, is perfect for patterns. It is light enough to cut with scissors, sturdy enough to withstand repeated use, and it doesn't stick to dough like rough cardboard. Scissors, mat knife or X-acto knife and straight edge (or metal-edged ruler) are used to cut out patterns. Use scissors for curves, mat knife or straight edge for straight lines, whenever possible.

How to Make Patterns

Full-sized patterns, some with fold lines, are given for each project. The number of cookies needed, thickness of dough required (if other than the assumed ¼″) and other information is marked. Label and transfer this information onto your pattern. They should be traced to make cardboard patterns for cutting out your cookies. A cardboard pattern, rather than a flimsy paper one, produces a more accurate shape and can be used many times.

Remember to place a cutting board underneath your work to protect your furniture from nicks. Lightly flour all patterns before use.

You will need tracing paper (to allow design to show through), carbon paper, scissors, a mat or X-acto knife and a pencil. A metal straight edge or metal-edged ruler is helpful for all straight lines.

To make patterns, place sheer paper over design in book and trace all lines. Place carbon paper, shiny side down, on cardboard and place drawing over that. Retrace all lines in order to transfer them to cardboard. Cut out pattern. Label and transfer printed information. Study pattern and choose a few major lines (to help decorate the baked cookie) such as belts, face outline, saddles, etc. Pierce them through the cardboard with an ice pick every ¼″ from front to back. (See diagram.) The ice-pick holes should leave a faint mark on the baked cookie when pressed on raw dough after the cookie is cut out. Partial lines could also be cut out with the mat knife, but be careful not to cut the pattern in half. Cut out all windows and doors.

PUNCH HOLES ON MAJOR LINES

How to Construct Bases

Most large projects presented here need a base. Gingerbread bases need an additional base underneath for support. Choose and prepare your base before you start the project, if possible. For a house or castle it gives portability and allows room for a festive setting. For other projects, it is simply protection for your furniture or woodwork. Sometimes just a thin sheet of clear plastic, cut to fit, will be sufficient to provide unobtrusive protection.

The base itself can be decorative and add to the sum of the project's parts. Some suggestions are: trays, plates, fabric or foil-covered cardboard, iced styrofoam, shallow baskets and boxes, 1/4″ plastic, plywood and masonite. I often use plastic and masonite rectangles (with little rubber feet) that my brother makes for me.

How to Light a Cookie House

This is a wonderful finishing touch that will get ooh's and ah's. To make this base you will need a masonite, plywood or plastic rectangle large enough to hold the house and trimmings. In addition, you will need a porcelain socket, a 2-strand electrical cord and plug, electricians' tape, glue, 4 small (1/2-1″) rubber or wooden feet (spools, scraps of wood, etc.), and a 15-watt light bulb.
1. Decide where the house will be on the base, and mark the outlines. Cut a 1″ hole at the center point.

2. On the underside of the base, glue the feet about 2″ in from corners.
3. Wire cord to socket and feed it through hole. Attach plug to end of electrical cord.
4. Place socket over hole and tape, glue or wire securely. Screw in bulb.
5. Generously pipe Royal Icing on lines. Immediately set house in position. Allow to dry thoroughly. Plug in cord.

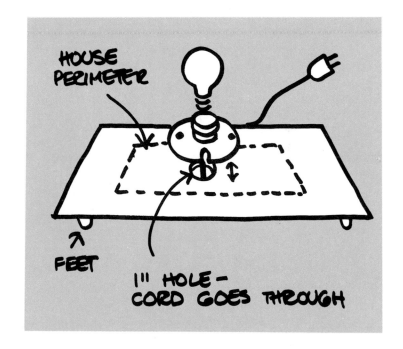

HOUSE PERIMETER

FEET

1″ HOLE - CORD GOES THROUGH

Recipes for Cookies and Icing

Cookies

Here are five easy recipes for gingerbread cookies that are deliciously fragrant.

The dough is so simple to make that it is suitable for children to use. Most recipes in this book call for five spices to help give color, flavor and scent to the dough. They are cinnamon, cloves, ginger, nutmeg and cardamom. If spices are less than a year old, they should still be fragrant, but they do not last forever. The freshness affects the gingerbread's taste and sweet smell tremendously. If your spice has just a slight smell, it will have little effect on the final product. While ginger is essential for true gingerbread, and cinnamon and cloves are important, the cardamom and nutmeg can be substituted with mace, allspice, pumpkin pie spice and grated orange or lemon peel.

Molasses varies in sweetness, density, color and flavor. I always use the well-known brands. Blackstrap molasses has not been used in this book but feel free to experiment. If you use it, you may need to add a little more sugar. Also, it will produce a darker dough.

Flour varies as well. Use all-purpose flour, not self-rising or Wondra. Partial whole wheat substitutions are suggested in two recipes only. The humidity in your area and the season affect the stickiness of the dough. Making gingerbread is not an exact formula, so you may have to add only a hint of flour if you live in a tropical paradise.

Brown (light or dark) or granulated sugar can be used interchangeably. The color of the sugar, affects the color of the dough. Raw or demerara sugar was not used for the book, but I do not anticipate problems if used. Do not substitute honey for the sugar, however, since the ratio of flour will change.

Margarine was used for the Architectural Dough, and butter was used for the regular Gingerbread Dough. Solid shortening may be used, but do not use oil as a substitute.

Mix all the cookie dough on low or medium speed, or by hand to avoid "fluffiness." At the end, when the last bit of flour has been added, the dough is stiff, and the mixer balks, you may use a metal spoon (a wooden one may break) or your immaculately clean hands.

Chilling the dough helps relax the flour's gluten and gives you time to make patterns, or even relax. All scraps may be re-rolled and used. For Architectural Dough leftovers, I recommend thin (⅛″ or ¹⁄₁₆″) cookies, since the dough produces a hard, crisp texture.

All measurements are given using standard measuring spoons and cups. Flour should be scooped and leveled off with a knife.

Baking time affects the color and dryness of the cookies. All Architectural Dough projects should be slightly overbaked and browned to ensure a rigid cookie that will stand up without bending.

Architectural Dough

Excellent, versatile dough suitable for building houses and other three-dimensional projects. It produces a hard cookie. Roll leftover dough very thin for crisp wafers.

1½ cups margarine or butter (3 sticks) or solid shortening
2¼ cups granulated or brown sugar
1½ teaspoons salt
1½ teaspoons baking soda
7 teaspoons ground ginger
4 teaspoons ground cinnamon
2 teaspoons ground cloves
2 teaspoons grated nutmeg (freshly grated, if possible)
1 teaspoon ground cardamom
1½ cups molasses, dark or light
½ cup water
7-8 cups all-purpose flour (*not* Wondra or self-rising)

In a large mixing bowl, cream margarine and sugar. Blend in salt, soda and spices. Stir in molasses and water. Add 4 cups flour (I use a 4-cup measure—it is a breeze this way), mix thoroughly. Stir in remaining 4 cups flour, a cup or so at a time until well mixed. Divide in half, wrap in plastic wrap and chill or freeze. Bake cookies on lightly greased sheets in preheated 350° oven until brown, about 10–20 minutes. Cool on wire racks. Makes two 14″ × 16″ rectangles, ¼″ thick.

Mini Recipe for Architectural Dough

In case you run out of dough and just want a *tiny* bit more, the division has been done for you. Makes one 7″ × 8″ rectangle, ¼″ thick.

6 tablespoons margarine (¾ of a stick)
½ cup granulated or brown sugar
½ teaspoon baking soda
½ teaspoon salt
1½ teaspoons ground ginger
1 teaspoon ground cinnamon
½ teaspoon ground cloves
½ teaspoon grated nutmeg (freshly grated, if possible)
¼ teaspoon ground cardamom
⅜ cup molasses, dark or light
2 tablespoons water
2 cups all-purpose flour (not Wondra or self-rising)

Follow the instructions for the Architectural Dough using the amounts given above.

Color Variations for Special Effects

LIGHT DOUGH: Substitute light corn syrup or honey for the molasses. The spices will lightly color the dough. The dough itself will be a little bit stickier, so it may take extra flour to work with the dough. This dough is not quite as flavorful as the ones with molasses.

DARK DOUGH: Use dark molasses and dark brown sugar when making dough. Extra ground cloves will darken dough. Longer baking time darkens cookies as well.

Gingerbread Dough

A spicy, classic dough for tender, delicious cookies meant simply for eating. It is not suitable for building houses. If you prefer a mildly spiced dough, use only 1 teaspoon of ginger and ½ teaspoon of cinnamon instead of the amounts given.

  - ¾ **cup butter or margarine (1½ sticks)**
  - ¾ **cup granulated or brown sugar**
  - 1 **teaspoon salt**
  - 1 **teaspoon baking soda**
  - 2 **teaspoons ground ginger**
  - 1½ **teaspoons ground cinnamon**
  - ½ **teaspoon ground cloves**
  - ½ **teaspoon grated nutmeg**
  - ¼ **teaspoon ground cardamom, optional**
  - ¾ **cup molasses**
  - ¼ **cup water**
  - 3¼ **cups all-purpose flour* (not Wondra or self-rising)**

Cream butter and sugar. Add salt, soda and spices. Stir in molasses and water. Gradually mix in flour until completely blended. Wrap and chill dough for 2 hours. Dough may be frozen at this point. Roll out dough, half at a time, and cut out cookies. Bake on lightly greased cookie sheets in preheated 350° oven until light brown around edges, about 10 minutes. Remove to cooling rack. Makes approximately 8 gingerbread boys and girls, ¼″ thick, using patterns on pages 69–72.

*1 cup of whole wheat flour can be substituted here.

Ginger Shortbread

A crisp cookie that can be iced. Not suitable for houses.

  - 1 **cup butter**
  - ½ **cup sugar**
  - ½ **teaspoon salt**
  - 2 **teaspoons ginger**
  - 2 **cups all-purpose flour* (not Wondra or self-rising)**

Cream butter, sugar, salt and ginger together. Stir in flour. Chill if desired. Roll ¼″ thick and cut out cookies. Place on ungreased cookie sheet and bake about 20 minutes in preheated 325° oven. Makes approximately 6 gingerbread boys and girls, ¼″ thick, using patterns on pages 69–72.

Icings

Here are five good recipes for different types of icing with suggestions for their use.

Royal Icing

Edible Royal Icing used throughout the book is ideal to decorate cookies when a hard finish is desired. This is the icing to use, like glue, when building houses and 3-D projects. Meringue powder can be used to replace egg whites; follow manufacturer's instructions and recipes. Do not overbeat the icing; it will become weak and difficult to work with. It's important to use grease-free utensils and bowl, otherwise icing will not peak properly.

  - 3 **egg whites**
  - ½ **teaspoon cream of tartar**
  - 1 **box (1 pound or approximately 3½-4 cups) confectioners' sugar, sifted**
  - ½ **teaspoon orange or lemon extract, optional**

*Can substitute half whole wheat flour.

Mix all ingredients on low speed for two minutes, then 5 to 8 minutes on moderately high speed until it forms peaks with a spoon. If peaks do not form after maximum time, beat icing for a minute or two at a higher speed. This icing dries out quickly. Keep it covered with a damp cloth or tightly fitted lid. It is best to make a batch at a time. It can be frozen to be used later for bases, etc., but the quality diminishes. Tint icing with paste food colors using a clean toothpick to transfer colors.

Flow or Covering Icing

This is simply Royal Icing thinned *slightly* with water. The water creates the proper consistency to fill in outlines. Be careful not to thin frosting too much, since it will look flat and lose its lustre. Check the consistency by dropping a bit from a spoon across the icing surface. The drop should take about three to four seconds to blend in. If it blends in immediately, it is much too thin; add some sifted sugar, a tiny bit at a time. Keep covered at all times.

Buttercream Icing

Tasty, creamy icing that is suitable for decorating cookies, but not strong enough to build with.

1 box (1 pound) confectioners' sugar
1 cup butter* (2 sticks)
¼ **teaspoon salt**
1 teaspoon orange or lemon extract
  About 2-3 tablespoons milk

Blend sugar, butter and salt together. Add extract and milk as needed until smooth. Do not make too thin. Makes about 2½ cups.

The following icings are designed primarily for leftovers. Since they aren't colored, they are not

*Can be half shortening.

as decorative as those already mentioned. If you wish, they can be piped on in a design.

Brandy Butter Icing

Use to ice decoratively-shaped gingerbread cookies. When icing is dry, the flavor of brandy is subtle.

½ **cup soft butter**
 2 cups confectioners' sugar
⅛ **teaspoon salt**
¼ **cup brandy (rum, amaretto and other liquors can be used)**

Cream butter, sugar and salt. Blend in brandy. Makes about 1½ cups or enough to ice about two dozen 3½" round cookies.

Variations

ORANGE BUTTER ICING: Orange blends well with the spices in gingerbread.
Substitute ¼ cup orange juice for brandy. Add 1 teaspoon grated orange rind. Makes about 1½ cups.

NUTMEG ICING: A flavor reminiscent of New England.
Substitute 2 tablespoons molasses and 3 tablespoons milk for the brandy. Stir in 1½ teaspoons freshly grated nutmeg, or to taste. Makes about 1½ cups.

How to Roll Out, Cut and Bake Cookies

Most rolled and cut cookies are prepared on a board or counter and then transferred to a baking sheet, altering cookie shapes in the process. The larger the cookie, the more distortion. For many cookies it is fine and even gives a homey, hand-made look to the cookies. Three-dimensional projects, such as houses, need lines and corners to be accurate. The straighter the lines, the easier it is to build a house.

This is simple to do by rolling dough, starting with one-half recipe at a time, directly on the lightly greased cookie sheet, then cutting out shapes and removing excess dough. Place a clean towel underneath cookie sheet to prevent slipping, and a piece of plastic wrap on top of dough. Or, instead of using plastic wrap, flour the rolling pin and roll out the dough.

Roll dough to desired thickness, using guides (if possible) at either edge of cookie sheet, not on the counter (dough would be rolled too thin). Dough can also be rolled between two sheets of plastic wrap, and then the whole piece can be transferred to the baking sheet before cutting. The thickness of the dough affects the yield. If you work without guides, you may find you have leftover dough or not quite enough. The Mini Recipe on page 17 is provided for this reason.

Cardboard patterns should be lightly floured, placed on dough and cut all around using a small sharp knife. Then remove the excess dough and keep scraps covered with plastic wrap.

Use patterns in descending order of size. The largest pattern should be cut when you have the largest amount of dough. Then use the next largest pattern until you need to use the other half of the dough. Reroll all scraps and continue cookie making in this manner.

The pattern pieces should be centered on the baking sheet with at least one inch between cookies to ensure even baking. Some patterns need to be flipped over. In other words a right and a left are needed, such as the side wall of

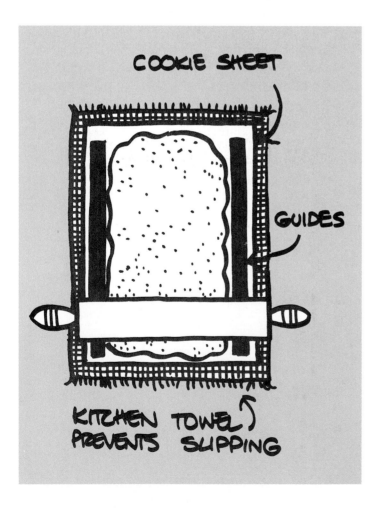

the Saltbox House. Specifications will be marked on the pattern. Projects such as the Rocking Horse, use 2 "rights" in their construction.

Most cookies will spread about ¼" all around and rise a bit. Chilling cut-out dough on cookie sheets helps cookies retain their shape and prevents spreading. If you are making a castle, for example, and want those jagged edges to be quite square, chill the dough about 10 minutes in the freezer or 15 minutes in the refrigerator, then bake immediately. The cookie will not rise or spread as much. Consistency throughout a project, with the exception of the train engine (baked over a juice can), insures that the pieces fit together correctly.

Another trick for geometric details, such as the jagged castle edge, is to leave a strip of excess dough to bake with the cookie. Recut the lines on the warm cookie and remove excess. (I eat this part!) This will prevent most cookie spread.

Similarly, windows and doors should be cut with the tip of a knife, baked intact and recut after baking. Windows can be removed from warm cookies, and they will cool evenly. Do not remove doors, because one end is open. Oddly enough, the lines will curve as they dry—so leave cut door in place until cookie has cooled thoroughly.

Most pieces are rolled ¼" thick and will puff up a bit during baking. It is a practical thickness that has an old-world look, and it is sturdy enough to hold up to young hands. Dough ⅛" thick seems fragile, and dough ½" seems a little chunky. Also, it takes twice as much dough much longer to bake. A ⅛" thickness is good for certain small details such as chimneys, and it is marked on patterns.

Large pieces, such as ¼"-thick house walls, will take longer to bake than smaller pieces of the same thickness. Cookies ⅛" thick will take about half the time. This is the general rule for ovens with an accurate temperature: a ¼"-thick

house wall will take about 18-20 minutes or longer to bake. A ¼"-thick cookie, such as a reindeer, will take about 10 minutes.

Cookies used for building should be slightly overbaked so that they will be strong and dry. They should be richly browned all over, but not burned at the edges. If you accidently burn the edges, cover them with icing or candy decorations later. Cookies meant solely for eating should be just lightly browned at edges for a more tender product.

Icing will help soften Architectural Dough cookies made from leftovers. After baking, let cookies cool a minute before transferring them to a cooling rack or brown paper. Loosen completely with a spatula. This is easy to do with small cookies, but the larger ones need special attention to prevent tearing. Let large cookies cool another minute or so. Hold cookie sheet at the same level as cooling rack, and gently slide cookie onto rack. Take care not to burn your

EXCESS DOUGH BAKED WITH COOKIE

COOKIE SHEET

fingers if the pan is still warm. (Another pair of hands would be helpful at this point.) Let cookies cool thoroughly before decorating—a two-hour minimum. If possible, let them sit overnight. Why rush something creative that is so much fun?

How to Make Candy Window Panes

Heat oven to 425°. Using a hammer, crush ⅓ cup hard yellow candy (such as lemon drops) between two sheets of wax paper. Crush to a uniformly fine powder, the consistency of sand. You may wish to finish the process in a blender or a food processor. On a foil-lined cookie sheet, spread candy powder in a 6″ × 6″ square ¼″ thick. Bake 3-5 minutes or until candy melts. Watch very carefully, since it burns easily. Remove from oven; let cool one minute. Using a large knife, divide candy into 9 2″ pieces. When cool, remove from foil. Stick to back of window with Royal Icing.

CUT MELTED CANDY INTO 9 PIECES

COOKIE SHEET

How to Decorate Cookies

This is the part everyone loves best—working with gloriously colored icing and candy to make the cookies spring to life. It is a little messy, but loads of fun. Work on a square of wax paper, and use it to turn cookies as needed.

Prepare Icing

Normally I use all white icing first, then the remainder is tinted as needed. Use a clean toothpick each time to transfer a dab of paste color to icing. Tinting pastels calls for restraint with the potent paste colors. Red is the opposite—it takes a lot of color and doesn't really taste very good. Stir icing to blend color.

Decorating Bag vs. Parchment Cone

You have two options for decorating bags. One is a plastic or cloth bag fitted with a metal decorating tip. The optional plastic couplers allow quick tip changes.

The advantage of the bag is that it holds a lot of icing. Therefore, it's great for covering large areas such as bases or big shapes. The disadvantages are that it has to be washed, it needs a tip for each bag and it is hard to use with a very small amount of icing. Clear plastic disposable bags are available.

The other option is the inexpensive parchment cone that is often used with no tip—just the point snipped off—and forms a nice line. The advantages are that it is disposable, a dozen colors can be in use at the same time because each bag is inexpensive, and it is easier to handle. Almost all my cookie decorating is done with parchment cones. Each is formed from a flat triangle—a simple procedure.

To Prepare a Decorating Bag

Drop a metal tip into the bag and push it down as far as it will go. If metal does not show all around, remove it and trim the end of the bag 1/8" at a time until tip clears bag edge by about 1/2". The bag is now ready to fill with icing. Remember you cannot change tips without removing icing unless you use a coupler.

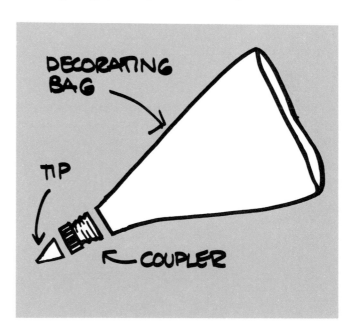

A coupler is a 2-part plastic device that allows you to change tips without removing the icing. If you have one, drop it into the bag and push it down as far as it will go. Use a pencil to mark coupler's last thread. Remove it and trim the bag at the pencil line. Insert coupler, place the tip over it and screw onto plastic bag. The bag is now ready to fill. Unscrew ring to change tips.

Hold bag midway and fold down top. Fill halfway *only* (too much icing will come out at the top). Unfold top and firmly twist bag closed.

To Prepare a Parchment Cone

1. Hold triangle with point up.

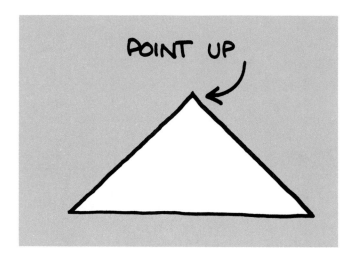

2. Roll in one corner (it doesn't matter which one), so that cone forms and corner matches point exactly.
3. Repeat with other corner.

4. Adjust as needed so that point is absolutely sharp.

5. Tape seam right up to point.

6. Fold in ends and you are ready to begin.

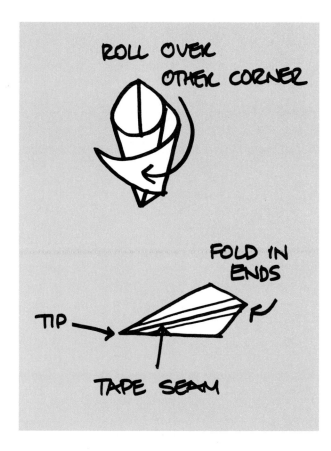

If you wish to use a metal tip, cut about ¾" off point and drop in tip. Push down for a snug fit. Or, snip about ¹⁄₁₆" off tip and squeeze out icing. Cut off more for a wider line.* Fill bag half full and fold down ends. Continue to fold down ends as you decorate.

*A ³⁄₁₆" line is approximately equivalent to a #3 tip's line.

Using the Decorating Bag or Parchment Cone

Hold and squeeze bag at top in your writing hand and apply gentle pressure just above tip with fingers of other hand. It may be helpful to rest forearm on a counter edge for stability.

Bag is usually held at a 45° angle for most decorating (except held at a 90° angle for Drop Flowers and Dots). Practice on wax paper. This will tell you how much pressure you need to get the look you want. The consistency of the icing is important. If it is not correct, the lines will not be graceful, but rather awkward.

Outlines and Writing

Outline the cookie first. Later fill in with flow icing where you want it. Use a #3 tip or equivalent for most projects and a #4 tip for larger ones. Hold bag at a 45° angle, touch tip to cookie and gently squeeze bag. Raise tip a bit and squeeze bag while directing tip around cookie. To finish a line, stop squeezing bag, touch tip to surface and pull up. Use this method for lines, curved or straight. Pipe all major lines such as faces and clothing. Let icing dry 20 minutes.

Filling in

To fill-in cookie, fill bag fitted with a #3 tip halfway with Flow Icing and close bag. Hold bag at a 45° angle and use a back-and-forth motion while squeezing bag to cover area with icing. It should sink in together and form a solid, flat opaque surface, which is slightly rounded.

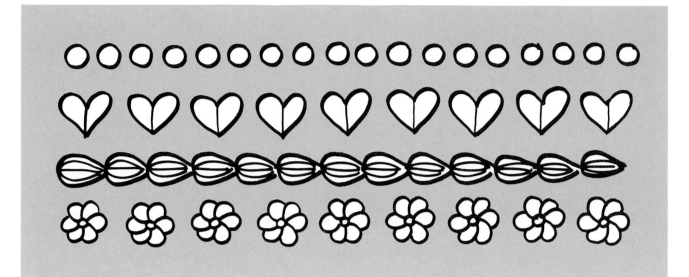

Special Effects

DOTS: These can be made separately on wax paper, allowed to dry 24 hours and peeled off. Adhere to cookie with Royal Icing. Dots are used for eyes as well as for decoration. When dropped on just-iced surface, flat "polka-dots" occur. Use a round #3 or #4 tip and hold bag at a 90° angle. Hold tip just above surface, squeeze bag until desired size is obtained, release pressure and pull tip away.

HEARTS: Best made ahead of time on wax paper and allowed to dry. Hold bag with a #3 or #4 tip at a 45° angle and make a dot. Relax pressure and pull tip towards the bottom of a small "V". Repeat for other side.

SHELLS: Use a #12 or #14 tip (both have serrated edges). Hold bag at a 45° angle with tip just above surface. Squeeze with pressure and lift tip up slightly to form a base. Relax pressure and pull tail towards you. Release pressure and pull up tip. Cover part of tail with next shell.

DROP FLOWERS: These bits of color are used throughout the book and are best made ahead on wax paper and allowed to dry. Use a #225 or #190 tip (two of many available) and Royal Icing of slightly stiffer consistency (add a bit more sifted confectioners' sugar). Hold bag at a 90° angle with tip touching surface, twist wrist around to left (or right). Apply pressure to bag as you untwist to form petals. Stop pressure and pull away. It will take a little practice. Add a dot of contrasting color at the center with a #3 tip.

How to Assemble Projects

The secret here is time and support. Time to let one section dry before adding another, and the support of heavy jars to hold cookies in position. A bag with a #3 tip is perfect for icing edges by running a bead or two of icing down. I often put projects together, such as the castle, with brown colored icing so that it is almost invisible. Then white icing can be neatly piped over it, if you wish.

A general rule was used for these patterns. Joints or seams were kept away from the front as much as possible. All house fronts and backs, for example, cover the side edges. Believe it or not, this affects the final shape of the house. Always check the photographs to make sure of construction.

Let's build a house step-by-step on a sheet of wax paper: have about 6 heavy jars standing by. These instructions should be used as a guide for all projects.

1. Start with back wall first. Place a jar on either side for support.
2. Ice back edge of one side wall and press to back wall. Use a jar for support wherever needed.
3. Repeat for other side wall.
4. Ice front wall edges and press house front into position. Make sure that corners are square; support wall with a jar.
5. If possible, squeeze icing inside house along seams for additional strength. Let dry overnight.
6. Remove jars at side walls. Ice upper edges

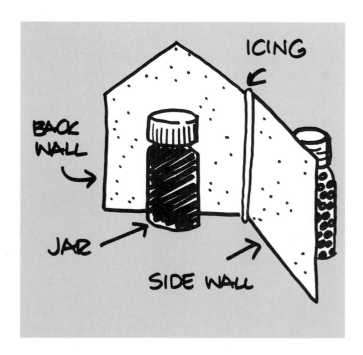

on one side of house, and place one roof piece in position. Support edge with jars or cans, stacked as needed.

7. Repeat for other side. Pipe icing neatly along peak. Add candy decoration at this point. Let dry 24 hours and it is ready.

How to Store Projects

Gingerbread projects can be eaten right away or stored for a year or two. Humidity is their main enemy. Gingerbread is traditionally baked during cold weather. It stays crisp and rigid in heated homes, too. To protect your lovely work during storage, several steps can be taken:

1. For houses, support the walls and roof with cardboard or foamcore board,* cut ¼″ narrower at sides and attach with Royal Icing.
2. Wrap house in plastic—large bags work best.
3. Set house inside a cardboard box, or place box over it (tie string over box to prevent accidents). The box will absorb some of the humidity.
4. Store box away from light and heat.

Please do not eat any old cookies. Though they may still be fragrant they will not taste very good, and they may not be good for you.

*Available in some art stores.

Teddy Bear Family

Everybody loves teddy bears. Teddies go on picnics, to birthday parties and even baby showers. Making teddy bears is easy. Colored outlines and partial icing fill-ins bring them quickly into your home. This style can be used for many cookies.

1 batch Gingerbread
    Dough
1 batch Royal Icing
1 Drop Flower per Mama
    Bear

Golden brown paste food
    color
#3 or #4 tip

1. Please read the general directions on pages 10–19. Make cookies and icing.
2. Use a #3 or #4 tip to outline bears with a light golden brown icing. Outline clothes in white. Let dry about 20 minutes.
3. Use a #3 tip and tinted Flow Icing to fill-in areas of color. Add black dots for eyes and nose.

Use golden brown icing for the mouth. Mama Bear's polka dots and necklace are made first on wax paper, then transferred and attached with Royal Icing.
Yield: 1 batch Gingerbread Dough makes 5 cookies.

PAPA BEAR

MAMA BEAR

BABY BEAR

Royal Castle

The fairy-tale image of a castle evokes magical settings. It can stand regally on its own with iced turrets, or it can be richly decorated with bright candy-covered turrets and brightly outlined wall edges. This is the largest project in the book and, with the exception of the zigzag edge, is not difficult to make because the components are simple. The fancy jagged edge may be replaced with a plain edge and evenly spaced sugar cubes. The turrets are quickly made of stacks of cookies iced together. Allow several days drying time.

3 batches Architectural Dough
3 batches Royal Icing
   14″ × 14″ piece heavy light blue metallic oaktag or board
   18″ × 18″ base or larger
7 ice cream sugar cones
3 pink-striped candy canes

28 Drop Flowers in assorted colors flags on toothpicks
3 Sky blue, violet, golden yellow and leaf green paste food colors
   2″ and 1½″ round cookie cutters (use pattern if not available)
   #2, #3, #12, #14 tips

1. Please read the general directions on pages 10–19. Make cookies and icing.

2. Prepare base. Secure a 14″ × 14″ piece of blue metallic oaktag to center of base with a thin layer of icing at center and edges. This will be the moat.

3. Prepare towers: Tint brown one-half batch of icing to match gingerbread. Use the best looking 56 two-inch cookies you have, and put together in stacks of 7 with a dot of icing in between cookies. Join 2 seven-cookie stacks together with icing. Place all four stacks on their sides, ends resting on a perpendicular surface such as a wall or backsplash. Lay a ruler across the stacks and press all to the same height, approximately 6″. Hold ruler in place with jars until dry. Repeat procedure for smaller cookies, making 2 stacks of 9 cookies (approximately 5″ high)

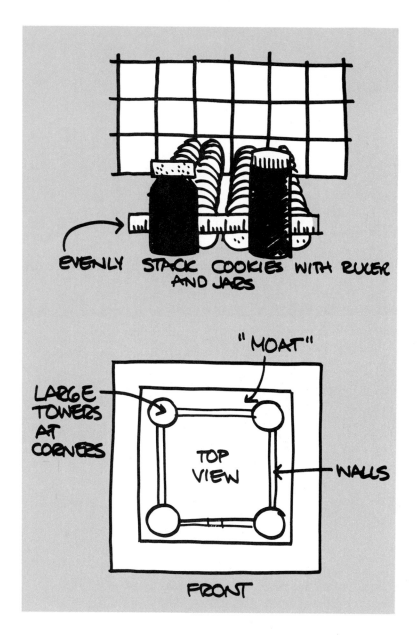

EVENLY STACK COOKIES WITH RULER AND JARS

"MOAT"

LARGE TOWERS AT CORNERS

TOP VIEW

WALLS

FRONT

and one stack with 11 cookies (approximately 5¾″ high). Save extras.

4. Decorate a small three-sided cookie with 3 dots of violet icing. Pipe a crown on small diamond-shaped cookie with golden yellow. A #2 tip works well for both.

5. With brown icing, attach front gate to front wall aligning doorways. Attach violet cookie to cover point. Press on crown cookie in upper half of front.

6. Working on the blue moat, place a large tower in each corner. Ice edges of back wall and press to vertical centers of back towers. Repeat process for front wall. Ice edges of side walls and push front and back units together to form a square in the center of the moat. Neatly pipe icing inside at base to secure castle to moat. Let dry thoroughly.

7. Put together 4 walls of lower base with brown icing. Add windows and cut-out door from front gate. When dry, ice bottom edges and place in the middle of the four outer walls.

8. Put together 4 upper walls of the second story of castle on its base with brown icing. When dry, ice upper edges of lower base, center middle unit and press into position.

9. Form third-story structure with 4 tower walls on its base with brown icing. Add windows. When dry, ice bottom edges and place in position at back of middle base. Place an empty juice can or its equivalent inside tower. Stack 3 two-inch cookies together, ice bottom cookie and place on top of can. Attach 11-cookie tower to top cookie. Add remaining 9-cookie towers in front corners.

10. Decorate turrets: Trim three ice cream cones to 3½″ with a serrated knife. Place cones upside-down on wax paper. Tint remaining batch of icing pale blue. Ice cones with spatula and let dry. Prepare a bag with a #14 shell tip and pipe four lines on each cone. (First, you may wish to mark each cone into quarters with a knife gently rubbed on the surface.) When cones are dry (about 24 hours), ice bottom edges and place on towers—the large cones go on the large towers, the smaller cones go on the smaller upper towers. Pipe a decorative border around base of each cone. Insert flags into tops of upper towers. Use more icing as needed.

11. Tint one batch of frosting light green. Using a #12 round tip, pipe a border of grass using a back-and-forth motion perpendicular to the edge of the base so that sides and front fuse. Fuse back to sides in the same manner. Just cover edge of moat and leave about 1″ of base edge showing. Trim three candy canes to fit from edge of grass to inside doorway, and set in place, side by side, on wet grass. Scatter flowers on grass, approximately seven per side.

Yield: 3 batches Architectural Dough makes one castle.

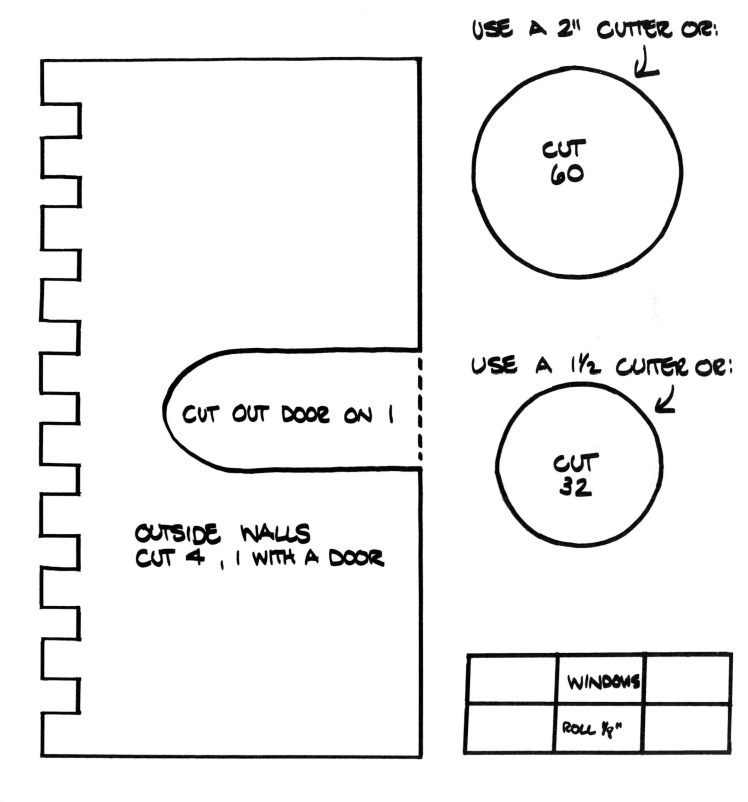

USE A 2" CUTTER OR:

CUT
60

USE A 1½ CUTTER OR:

CUT
32

CUT OUT DOOR ON 1

OUTSIDE WALLS
CUT 4, 1 WITH A DOOR

	WINDOWS	
	ROLL ⅞"	

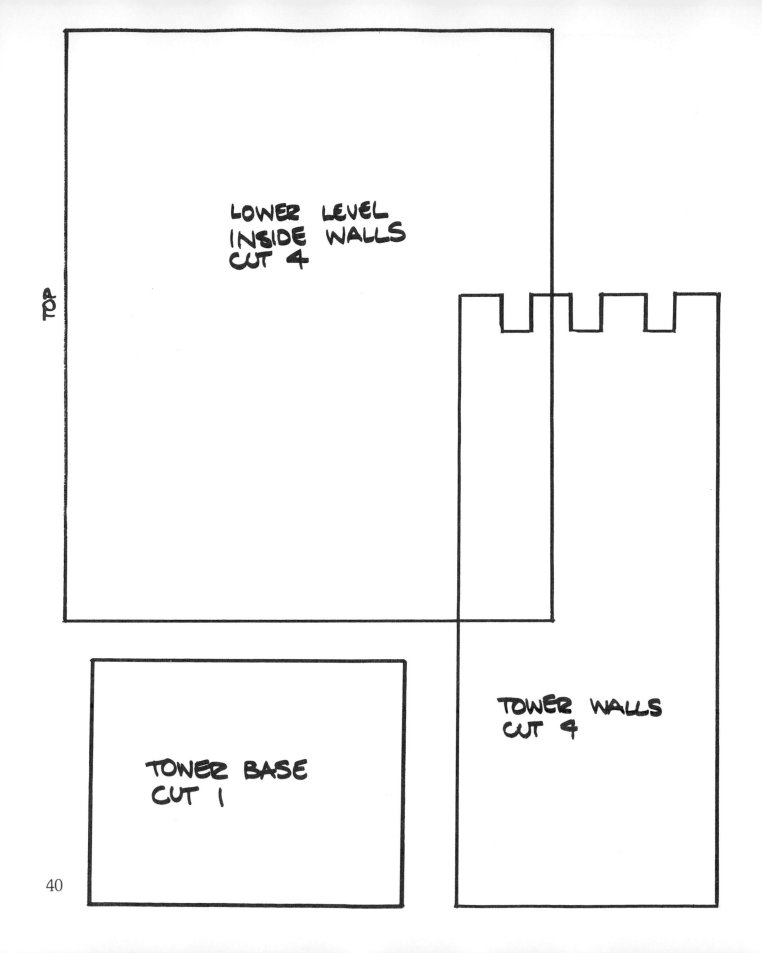

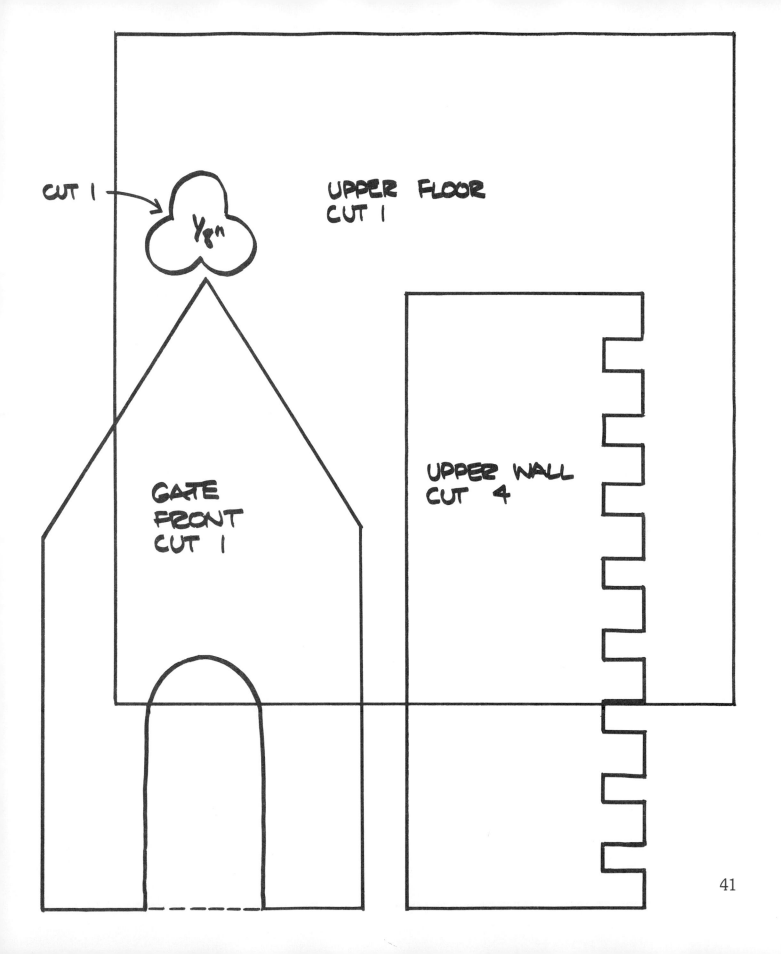

CUT 1

$\frac{7}{8}"$

UPPER FLOOR
CUT 1

GATE
FRONT
CUT 1

UPPER WALL
CUT 4

41

Musical Instruments

These three musical instruments are perfect bedtime snacks, as Christmas ornaments or even at your next recital. Should you want to create a larger orchestra, try your hand at designing other instruments.

1 batch Gingerbread Dough
1–2 batches Royal Icing (as needed)

Brown, red, and yellow paste food colors
#1, #3 tips

1. Please read the general directions on pages 10–19. Make cookies and icing.

2. With a #3 tip and brown icing, outline all major design details. Let dry 20 minutes. Tint ¼ remaining icing ivory. Use a #1 tip to pipe fine harp and violin strings.

3. Thin remaining icing to flow consistency. Tint half yellow for horn, and half red for harp. Use a #3 tip with back-and-forth motion to fill in colored areas.

Yield: 1 batch Gingerbread Dough makes 12 cookies.

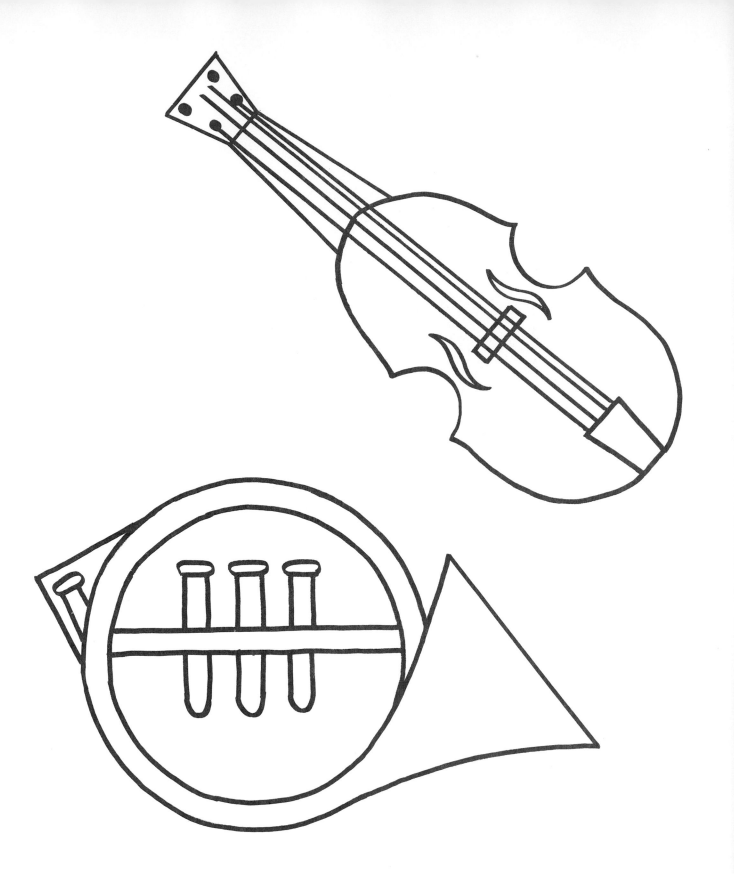

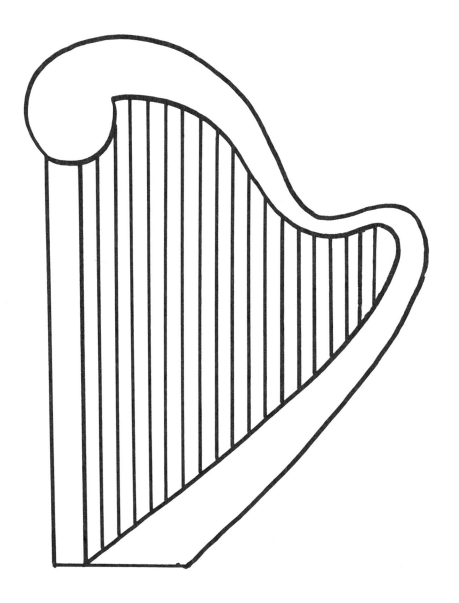

Valentine Hearts

A six-heart round, inspired by a colonial dish, is a perfect treat for a family or small group. Break off a heart on the scored line to serve individually (but don't break a heart!). Besides regular gingerbread dough, ginger shortbread works well with this shape. Decorate it with fork tines in the classic tradition.

1 batch Gingerbread Dough

1 batch Royal or Buttercream Icing, optional

Pink and leaf green paste food colors, optional

#3 tip

1. Please read the general directions on pages 10–19. Cut out cookie on baking sheet. Cut center lines, but leave cookie intact. Re-cut lines after baking almost all the way through.

2. Use a #3 tip to outline cookie and flowers in chosen colors. Let dry about 20 minutes.

3. Use the same tip and Flow Icing to fill in cookies.

Yield: 1 batch Gingerbread Dough makes 2 hearts.

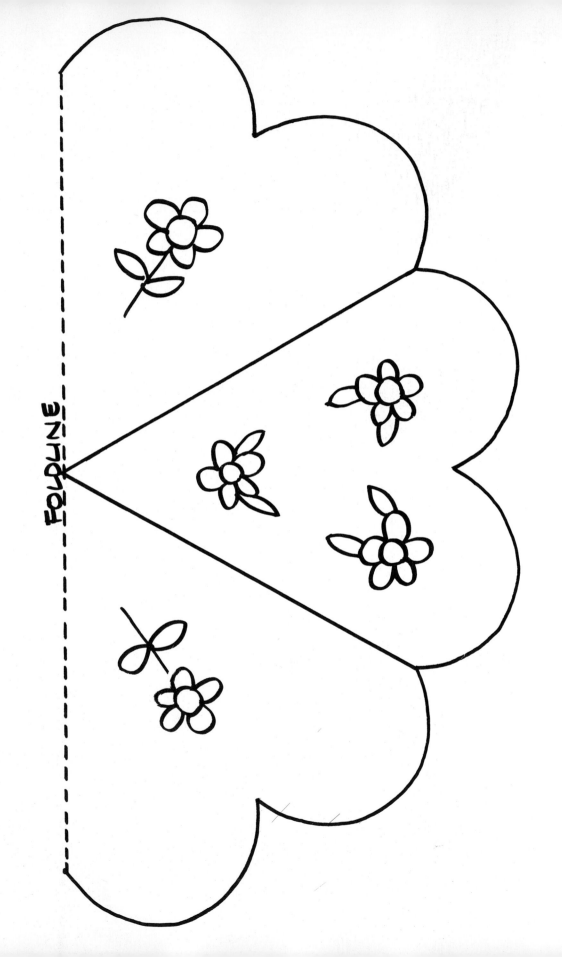

FOLD LINE

Polka-Dotted Easter Bunny

Delight a child with a sunny Easter bunny. This is a 10″ cookie wrapped in cellophane and tied with a ribbon—a great way to present flat cookies. Creating an Easter basket for the Bunny's gifts is easily accomplished by painting an inexpensive basket (with ordinary latex) and filling it with goodies.

1 batch Gingerbread
   Dough
1 batch Royal Icing
2 Drop Flowers

Assorted paste food
   colors, (aqua, leaf
   green, yellow, violet,
   pink)
#3, #4 tips

1. Please read the general directions on pages 10–19. Make cookies and icing.
2. Using a #3 or #4 tip (I used a #4 here), outline body, arms, egg and major lines in violet icing. Eyes, nose and mouth will be done later. Save bag in plastic wrap.
3. Thin remaining white icing to flow consistency. Use a #3 or #4 tip to fill in bunny. Tint small amounts of pastel colors to use with a tip to make polka-dots on wet icing. Dots will flatten. Pipe in egg colors. Let dry thoroughly.
4. Pipe on remaining details; add flowers.

Yield: 1 batch Gingerbread Dough makes 4 bunnies.

51

Halloween Party

On All Hallows Eve, witches and ghosts dance feverishly around a grinning jack o'lantern. Recreate this legend for your favorite goblins with the snaggle-tooth pumpkin centerpiece and spooky cookie designs featured here. This project is very simple, since all cookies are flat, including the pumpkin, which is supported by a cardboard triangle. The number of cookies you intend for goblin-gobbling will determine how much decorating is to be done.

1 batch Gingerbread
   Dough
1 batch Royal Icing
   Orange and black food
   colors

Candy corn
#3, #4 tips

1. Please read the general directions on pages 10–19. Make cookies and icing. Pumpkin can be made with Architectural Dough or Gingerbread Dough. Architectural Dough is sturdier.

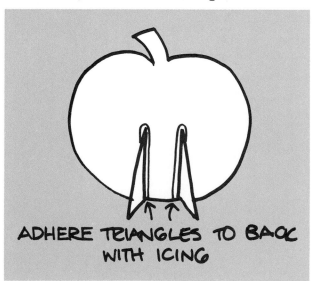

ADHERE TRIANGLES TO BACK WITH ICING

2. Use a #3 tip to outline major lines on all small cookies in the appropriate color; add candy corn to witch's nose. Make two white dots for eyes. Use a #4 tip to outline large pumpkin. Let dry 20 minutes.

3. Thin remaining frosting to covering consistency with a little water. With #3 tip, fill in ghost with white using a back-and-forth motion. Tint ¾ of the remaining icing orange; tint ¼ black. Fill in pumpkin eyes, nose and mouth in black. Use candy corn to make teeth. Pipe on ghost eyes and mouth with elongated dots. Pipe a dot of black on witch's eyes and a mole on chin; fill in hat. Finish decorating with orange icing.

4. Adhere triangles to large pumpkin.

Yield: 1 batch Architectural Dough makes 2 pumpkins. 1 batch Gingerbread Dough makes 8 cookies.

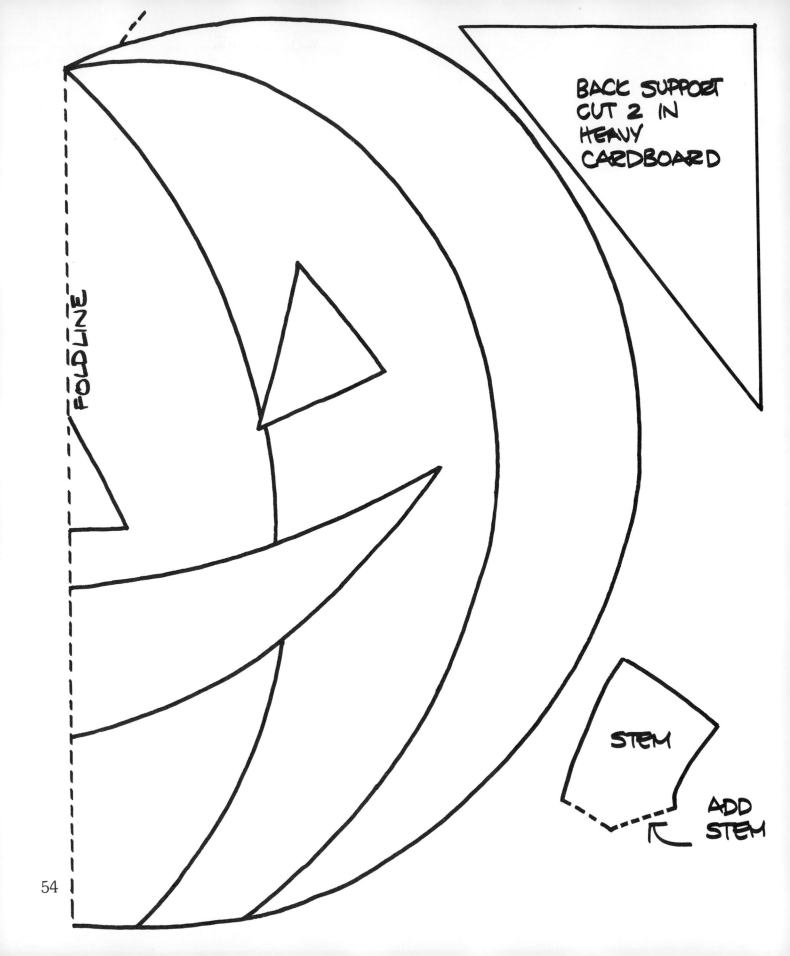

FOLD LINE

BACK SUPPORT
CUT 2 IN
HEAVY
CARDBOARD

STEM

ADD
STEM

54

FOLDLINE

The Pilgrim's Thanksgiving

This colonial setting, inspired by the first Thanksgiving, brings a festive centerpiece to your holiday feast. You may want to decorate the saltbox house sparsely with red lines and touches of white to evoke memories of the day when pilgrims in simple frocks gave thanks for a bountiful harvest. After you have completed the house and sprinkled candy to suggest autumn leaves, prepare Indian Corn Cookies to adorn the table as well. Once you have combined the centerpieces, Indian Corn Cookies, a selection of pumpkins and the roasted turkey, your table will be an appetizing delight deserving, like our pilgrim forefathers, great praise and thanksgiving.

2 batches Architectural Dough
2 batches Royal Icing
Candy corn

Brown, orange, red and yellow paste food colors
Base
#3 tip
Natural burlap to cover base
Foamcore board

1. Please read the general directions on pages 10–19. Make cookies and icing. Add ¼" all around to side wall pattern; cut one in foamcore. This will be used as a support.

2. For a decorating guide, score slat lines on all four house walls every ½" with a clear plastic ruler and a small sharp knife. This works best on a warm cookie.

3. Tint half of one batch of icing red; leave the rest white. Tint ¾ of the other batch of icing brown to match gingerbread; tint remaining icing yellow. After piping, tint leftover white icing orange.

4. Use a #3 tip and white icing to outline pilgrims, pumpkins, turkey, windows and door. Ice pumpkins orange. Ice window interiors and tur-

key tail feathers yellow. Use a #3 tip again to put red dots on turkey feathers, pumpkins and fill in window sashes. Pipe a red line on each score mark, then pipe another line between them so that lines are ¼" apart. Pipe bricks on chimney. Let dry thoroughly. Pipe window details in white.

5. Place roof pieces flat on counter. Tint remaining icing brown. Ice front roof. Overlap 7 roof strips evenly. Starting at lower edge of roof and working up, pipe icing on upper edge of each strip to hold the next one in place until you get to the last piece. Ice back roof and overlap 11 strips. Let dry thoroughly.

6. Assemble house with brown icing. Support back wall with heavy jars. Ice edges of side walls and press to back wall. Place front in position. Support with jars. Position supporting foamcore wall in the middle of the house. Trim foamcore so that it fits securely. Pipe icing at inside seams to hold in position. Let dry thoroughly.

7. Ice upper edges of all walls and place roof pieces in position. Support with tall jars, stacked as necessary. When set, ice bottom edge of chimney and place in center. Let dry 24 hours.

8. Cover base with burlap. Ice a thick line on base and set house on top. Ice small cardboard triangles to pilgrims and turkey so they will stand. Arrange the setting.

Yield: 2 batches Architectural Dough makes 1 house, 2 pilgrims, and 1 turkey.

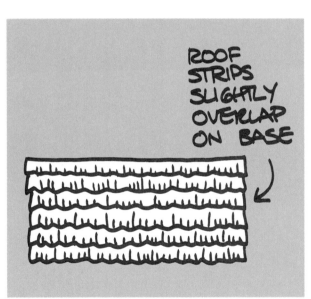

ROOF STRIPS SLIGHTLY OVERLAP ON BASE

SIDE WALL

ATTACH HOUSE HERE

60

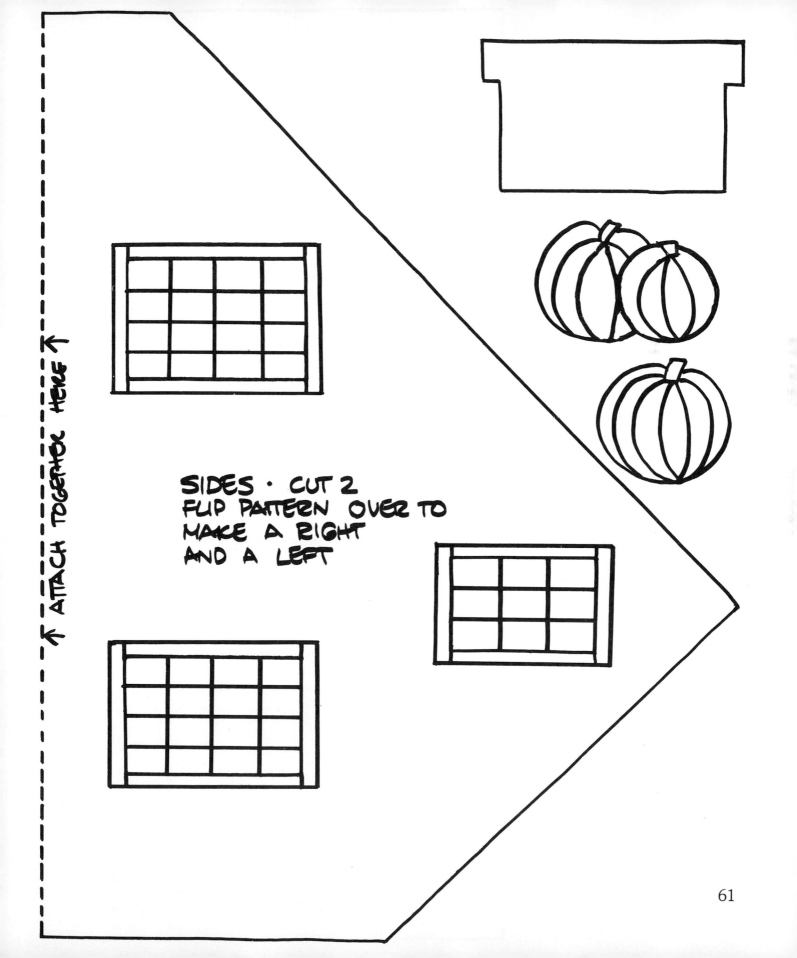

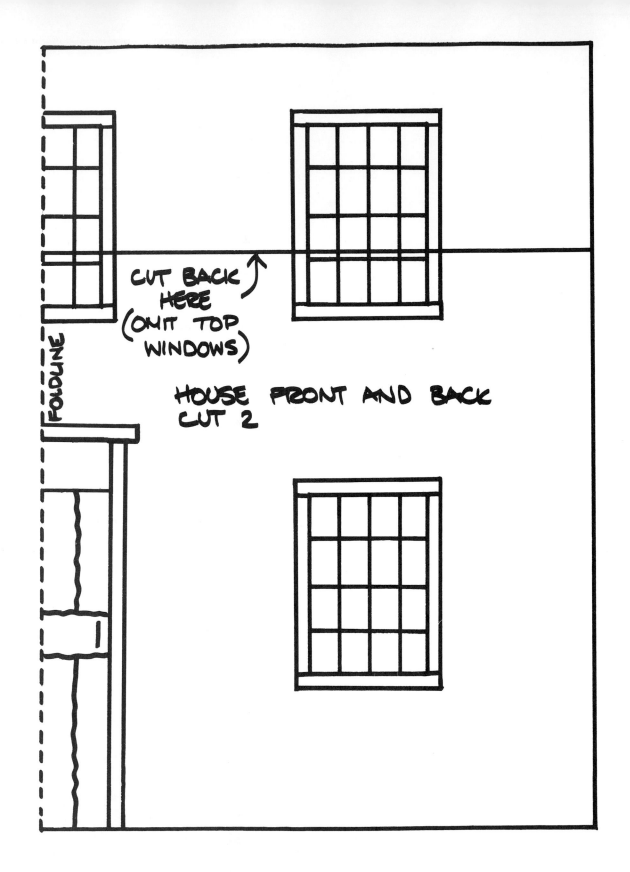

CUT BACK HERE
(OMIT TOP WINDOWS)

FOLDLINE

HOUSE FRONT AND BACK
CUT 2

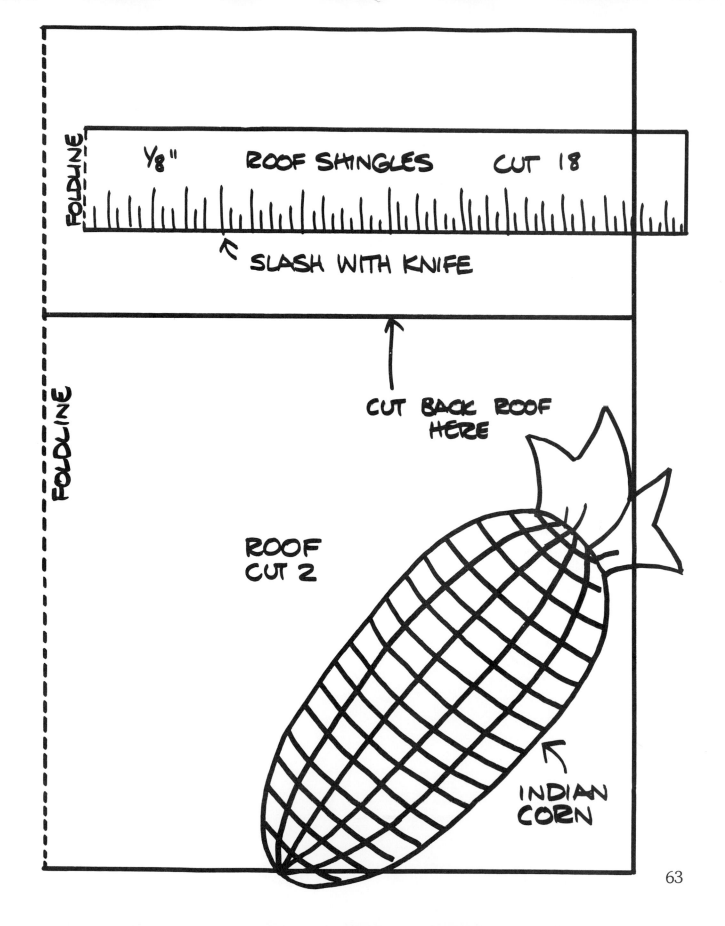

FOLDLINE

⅛" ROOF SHINGLES CUT 18

↑ SLASH WITH KNIFE

FOLDLINE

↑ CUT BACK ROOF HERE

ROOF CUT 2

↖ INDIAN CORN

Rag Dolls, Two Winter Kids, Little Lord and Lady, Farm Girl and Boy

The two basic cookie shapes are the gingerbread boy and girl, shown here in four different variations. The cookies can also be decorated in an old-fashioned manner with raisins and white icing. These simple patterns offer a limitless array of combinations. Several possibilities include: gingerbread families, cartoon characters and fairy tales.

1 batch Gingerbread Dough

1–2 batches Royal Icing
Assorted paste food colors
#2, #3 tips

1. Please read the general directions on pages 10–19. Make cookies and icing.
2. Working with a #3 tip and white icing, outline all major design details. Let dry 20 minutes or longer. Reserve about ½ cup icing for final finishing details and face design.
3. Thin remaining icing to covering consistency with drops of water. Tint as needed using photograph as guide.

4. Using a #3 tip, fill in areas of solid color with a back-and-forth motion. Let dry several hours between colors, if possible, to prevent smudges.
5. Work with a #2 or #3 tip to add eyes and mouth and finishing details to cookies, such as blouse tucks and buttons.

Yield: 1 batch Gingerbread Dough makes 8 characters.

GIRL

BOY

72

Cowboy and Country Miss, Prince and Princess, Santa and Mrs. Claus, Indian Brave and Squaw

Here are two more versatile cookie shapes, this time for adults. They are shown four different ways to inspire you. All can be coordinated with other projects. Prince and Princess cookies, for example, could be served at a party where the Royal Castle is the centerpiece. All these cookies, and the boys and girls as well, would make charming ornaments.

1 batch Gingerbread
  Dough
1–2 batches Royal Icing
  and Flow Icing
  (as needed)

Silver dragees for Indians
  and Prince
Assorted paste food colors
#2, #3 tips

1. Please read the general directions on pages 10–19. Make cookies and icing.
2. Use a #3 tip and white icing to outline all major design details. Let dry 20 minutes. Reserve approximately ½ cup icing for later use.
3. Use Flow Icing and a #3 tip to fill in areas with solid color.

4. Work with a #2 or #3 tip to add face details and other finishing trim with reserved icing.

Yield: 1 batch Gingerbread Dough makes 8 characters.

MAN

ADD
HAT →

79

WOMAN

← ADD PEAK
TO PATTERN

81

Santa and Sleigh

Cookies featuring Santa and his reindeer zooming through the starry night will be the delight of the holiday season. Santa and the reindeer are flat cookies, while the sleigh is three-dimensional. The reindeer could be made to stand one of three ways. The first is the same method used for the donkey and camel in the nativity scene: the legs are not cut out and a cardboard triangle supports from the back. Another method is to cut the legs out and make 2″ × 5″ bases for each reindeer, attached with icing. Or attach a small bar cookie that you've made, ½″ × 2″, in between the two deer. Any method makes for a very merry scene.

1 batch Architectural Dough
1 batch Royal Icing
   Narrow cord or ribbon, if you wish to connect reindeer with reins
   Red, green, yellow, pink and sky blue food colors

Multi-colored sprinkles
Silver dragees
#3 tip
1 cinnamon candy for Rudolph's nose

1. Please read general directions on pages 10–19. Make cookies and icing. Make a hole near Santa's hand with a drinking straw or chopstick, if you want him to hold the reins.

2. Use a #3 tip and outline all cookies and important design features such as saddles and clothing. Let dry 20 minutes. Ice antlers and dust with colored sprinkles.

3. Thin remaining icing to covering consistency. Fill in all white areas such as Santa's beard, etc. using a #3 tip and a back-and-forth motion.

4. Tint approximately ⅔ remaining icing yellow and fill in sleigh sides, back and front. Let dry thoroughly.

5. Tint a small spoonful of icing blue for Santa's eyes and another spoonful red for reindeer cheeks. All should be piped with a #3 tip.

6. Divide remaining icing in half—one part red, the other dark green. Fill in Santa's suit and hat, reindeer harnesses and parts of saddles. Fill in green; add silver dragees. Add finishing white trim to sleigh runners and sides.

7. When all is thoroughly dry, rest one sleigh side on counter, iced side up. Ice one edge of base and place on lower part of yellow section of sleigh. Ice sides and lower edges of front and back and press in position on sleigh sides and base. Let dry several hours. Ice front, back and base edges and place remaining side in position. Place between heavy jars for support and let dry overnight.

8. Finish reindeer and set up. A cord can be tied around each reindeer neck and run through the hole near Santa's hand.

Yield: 1 batch Architectural Dough makes 1 Santa, 1 sleigh and 12 reindeer.

COOKIE BAR SUPPORT
BETWEEN 2 DEER

ON A BASE
WITH ICING

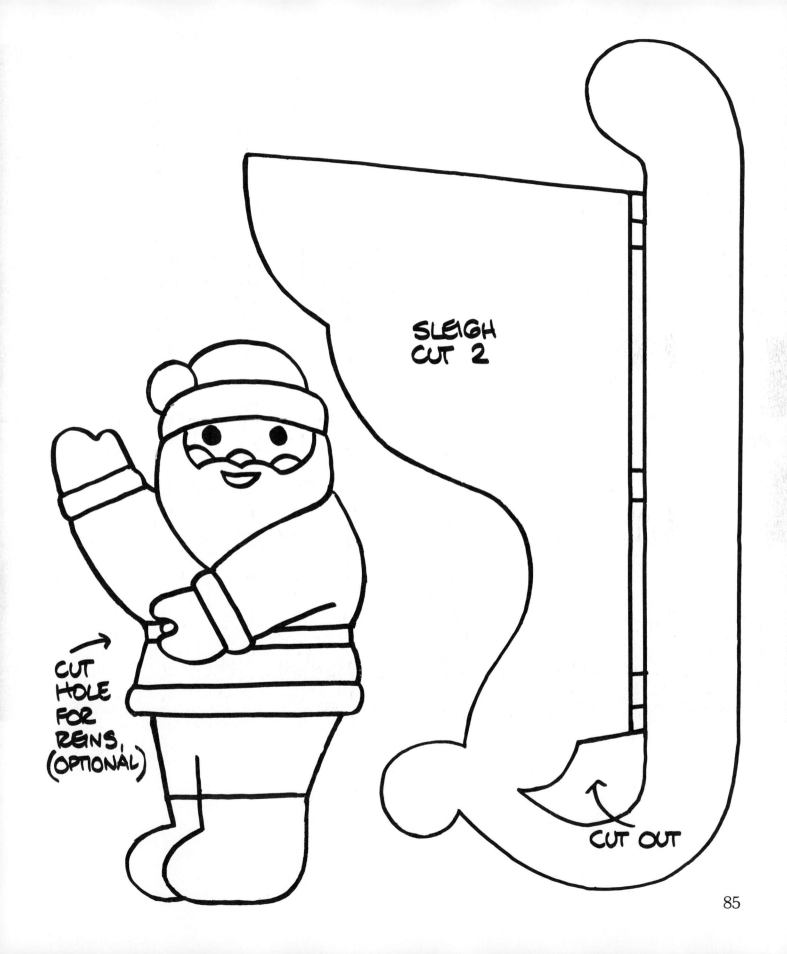

SLEIGH
CUT 2

CUT
HOLE
FOR
REINS,
(OPTIONAL)

CUT OUT

85

SLEIGH FRONT
CUT 1

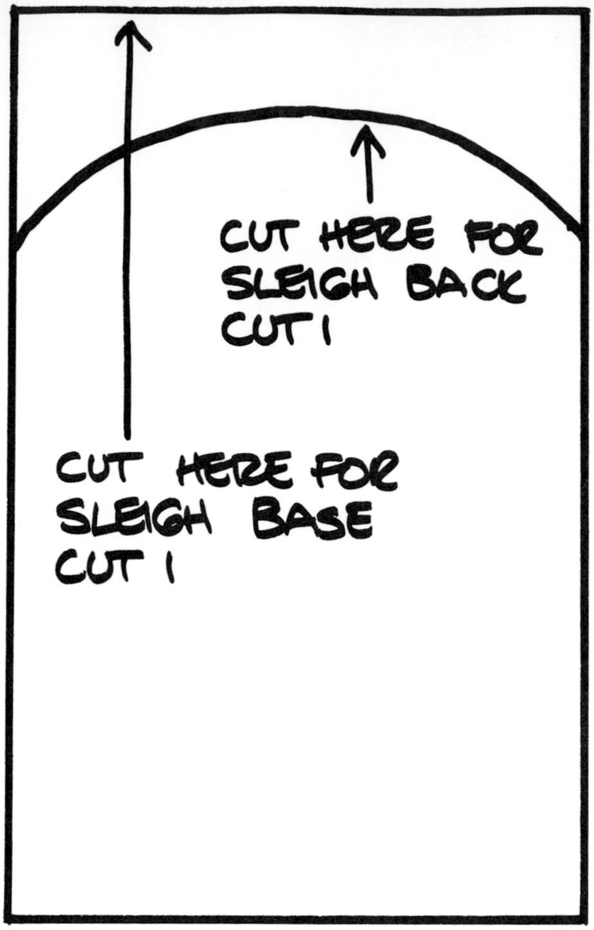

↑ CUT HERE FOR
SLEIGH BACK
CUT 1

CUT HERE FOR
SLEIGH BASE
CUT 1

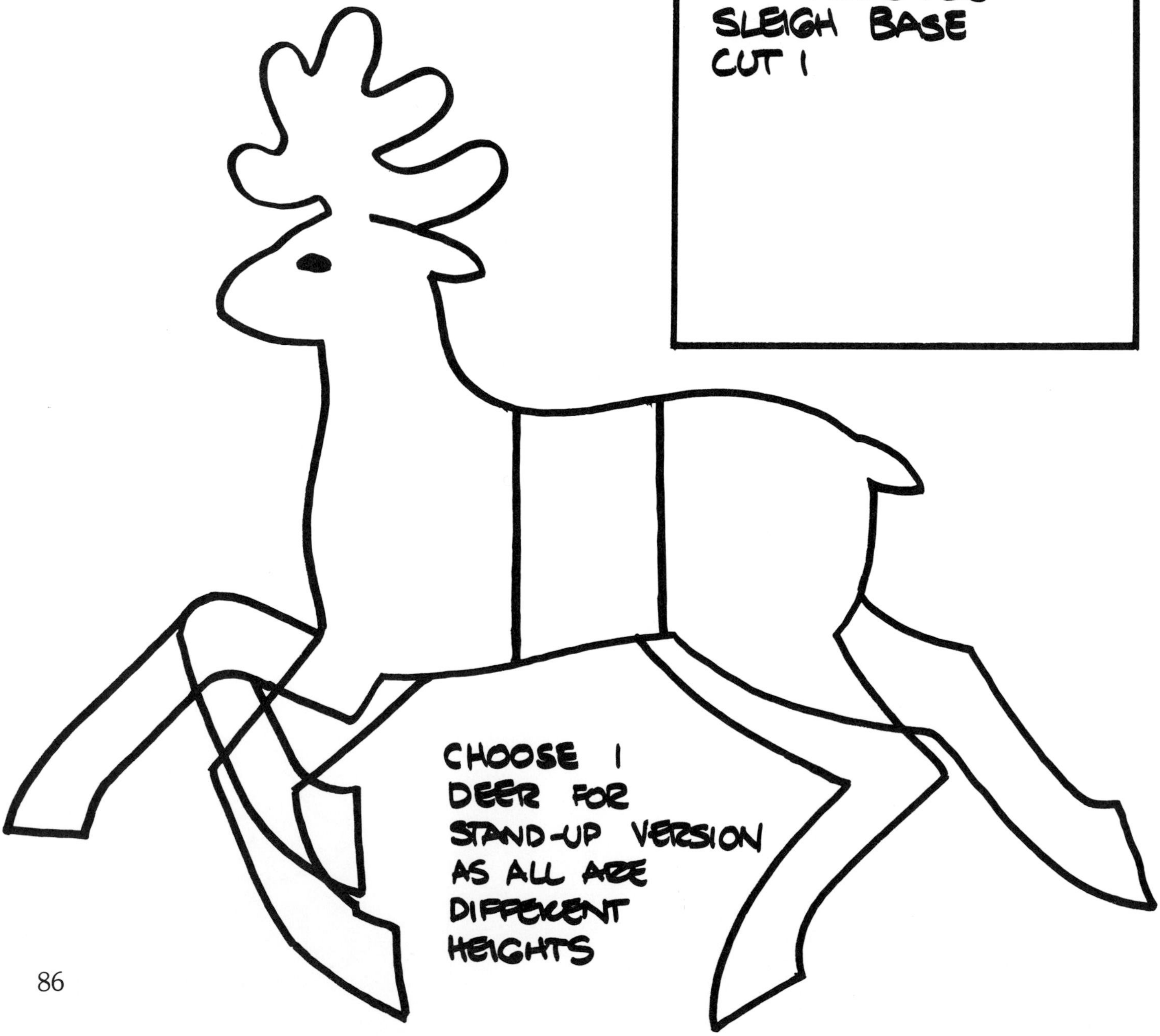

CHOOSE 1
DEER FOR
STAND-UP VERSION
AS ALL ARE
DIFFERENT
HEIGHTS

Santa's Stocking

After a long night of slipping down chimneys to bring toys to the world's children, nothing brings a smile to Santa's face like Mrs. Santa Claus' cookie nightcap. Tuck in your world-weary loved ones with this cellophane and ribbon-wrapped cookie, and monogram their name on the stocking like Mrs. Claus did. The cookie can be decorated with Christmas-colored icing to capture the holiday spirit.

1 batch Gingerbread Dough	Red, leaf green, sky blue food colors
1–2 batches Royal Icing and Flow Icing	Silver dragees
	#3 tip

1. Please read the general directions on pages 10–19. Make cookies and icing.
2. Pipe outline and key design elements (toe, heel, stripes) on cookie using a #3 tip and white icing. Reserve some icing to pipe name, greeting, snowflakes and toe and heel trim. Let dry 20 minutes.
3. Use Flow Icing to fill in all white areas first with a #3 tip. Put on silver dragees. Use photograph as a color guide. Divide remaining icing into thirds. Tint ⅓ green, ⅓ red and ⅓ blue. Fill in the solid areas. The tree trunks in middle strip are plain. Let dry several hours.
4. Use a #3 tip to pipe on name, toe and heel trim in red. Pipe snowflakes and greeting in white.

Yield: 1 batch Gingerbread Dough makes 3 stockings.

MERRY CHRISTMAS

Colonial Wreath

In Williamsburg, Virginia there are many appealing Christmas decorations made of fruit. This cookie wreath continues this colonial influence. It can be used as a wall hanging or candle wreath, if it is backed with cardboard to prevent grease marks. The base is rolled ¼″ thick as usual and the top cookies are rolled ⅛″ thick. All the pieces are decorated separately prior to final assembly.

1 batch Architectural
    Dough
1–2 batches Royal Icing
1 batch Flow Icing
    Red, orange, yellow,
      brown and leaf green
      food colors

6–8 Drop Flowers
    Brown corrugated
      cardboard
    #3, #4 tips

1. Please read the general directions on pages 10–19. Make cookies and icing.

2. Finish back of wreath before decorating. Trace base onto brown corrugated cardboard and cut out. Thickly coat back of wreath with icing and attach cardboard. If you wish, cover the back of the cardboard with a brown felt circle.

3. Tint a small amount of icing dark green. Use a #4 tip to outline base edges in green. Pine sprigs will be piped on after white areas are dry. Use a #3 tip and white icing to outline all fruit.

4. Make Flow Icing. Use a #4 tip and white icing to fill in solid area with a back-and-forth motion. Let dry thoroughly. Tint remaining icing, in five equal parts, red, dark lime green, orange, light brown and lemon yellow. Fill in fruit with solid areas of the appropriate color using a #4 tip. Let dry thoroughly.

5. Pipe pine sprigs following pattern guide, using a #3 tip and reserved dark green icing. Pipe brown stems and white highlights on apples and pears. Pipe dots on citrus fruit. Let all pieces dry thoroughly.

6. Assemble fruit and Drop Flowers in an appealing manner. Attach each piece, one by one, with a dab of icing. Let dry thoroughly. Tie ribbon around wreath.

Yield: 1 batch Architectural Dough makes 2 wreaths.

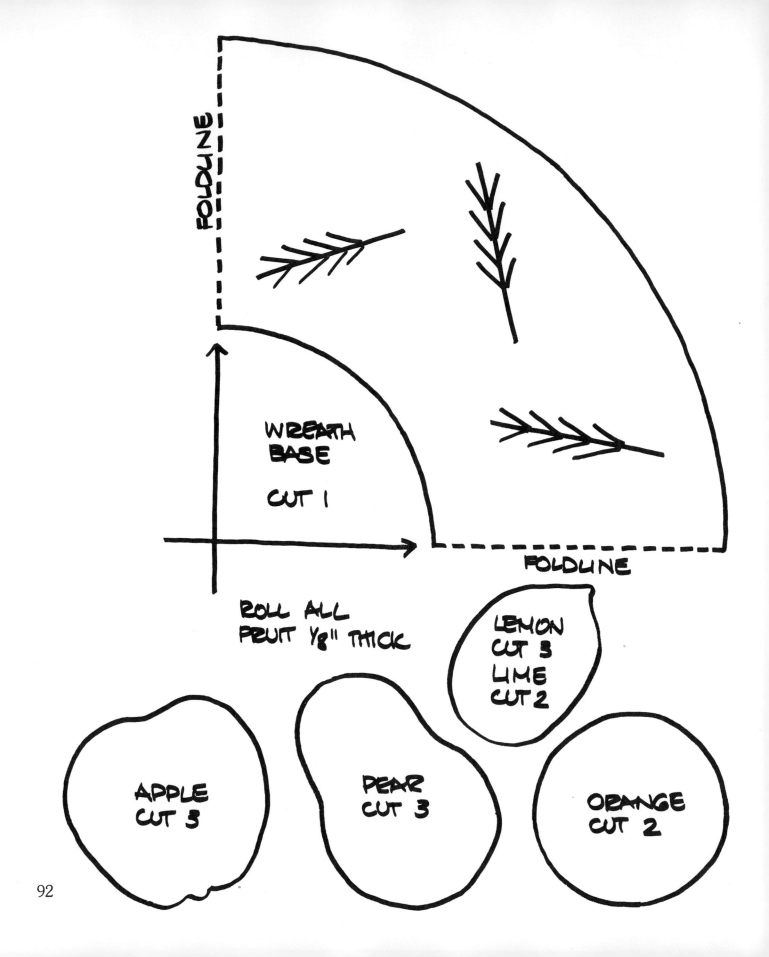

FOLDLINE

WREATH
BASE

CUT 1

FOLDLINE

ROLL ALL
FRUIT ⅛" THICK

LEMON
CUT 3
LIME
CUT 2

APPLE
CUT 3

PEAR
CUT 3

ORANGE
CUT 2

Gumdrop Express

This candy-studded choo-choo train is a suitable decoration for any happy occasion. Since the track is not very wide, it can be placed along bookshelves or atop a mantel. Each car is separate to facilitate construction, and the rounded surfaces of the engine can be baked over a small juice can. Or use the juice can to cut five ¼″ cookies that can be iced together to make your engine.

1 batch Architectural Dough
1 batch Royal Icing
    Star canapé cutter
2 large lollipops, sticks cut off (for engine wheels)

Red and yellow food colors
16 round, flat gumdrops for wheels
4 small candy canes
Assorted candy
#3 tip

1. Please read the general directions on pages 10–19. Make cookies and icing.

2. Make 6 star cookies ⅛″ thick. For juice can engine, use an X-acto knife or a sharp knife to trim a small juice can to 2½″. Cover with foil; tuck ends in. Cover can with cut dough and pinch seam together. Place seam side down on cookie sheet. Chill in freezer 10 minutes. Bake about 12 minutes until edges are brown. Do not remove can; it will act as a support. An easier technique would be to make 5–6 round cookies with juice cans and ice them together.

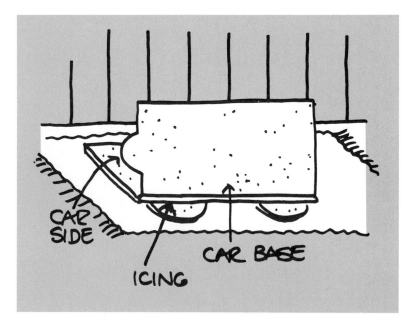

CAR SIDE

ICING

CAR BASE

3. Decorate all sides flat. Pipe windows in white with a #3 tip and fill in with bright yellow Flow Icing. Pipe on borders, etc. as you wish. Pipe front lines or cowcatcher. Attach round, flat gumdrops in wheel position.

4. The easiest way to assemble all cars is on their sides. Lay side piece on a soft, clean towel iced side down and attach car base to side; support with jars. Add front, back and other side piece.

5. Add roof to engine, ice it and add jelly beans. Ice caboose roof red and dip sides in sprinkles before attaching; add peppermints and chimney. Attach large lollipop engine wheels. Attach front piece to engine. Add cow catcher to front piece at slight angle. Add finishing touches and off she goes.

Yield: 1 batch Architectural Dough makes 1 train (tight fit).

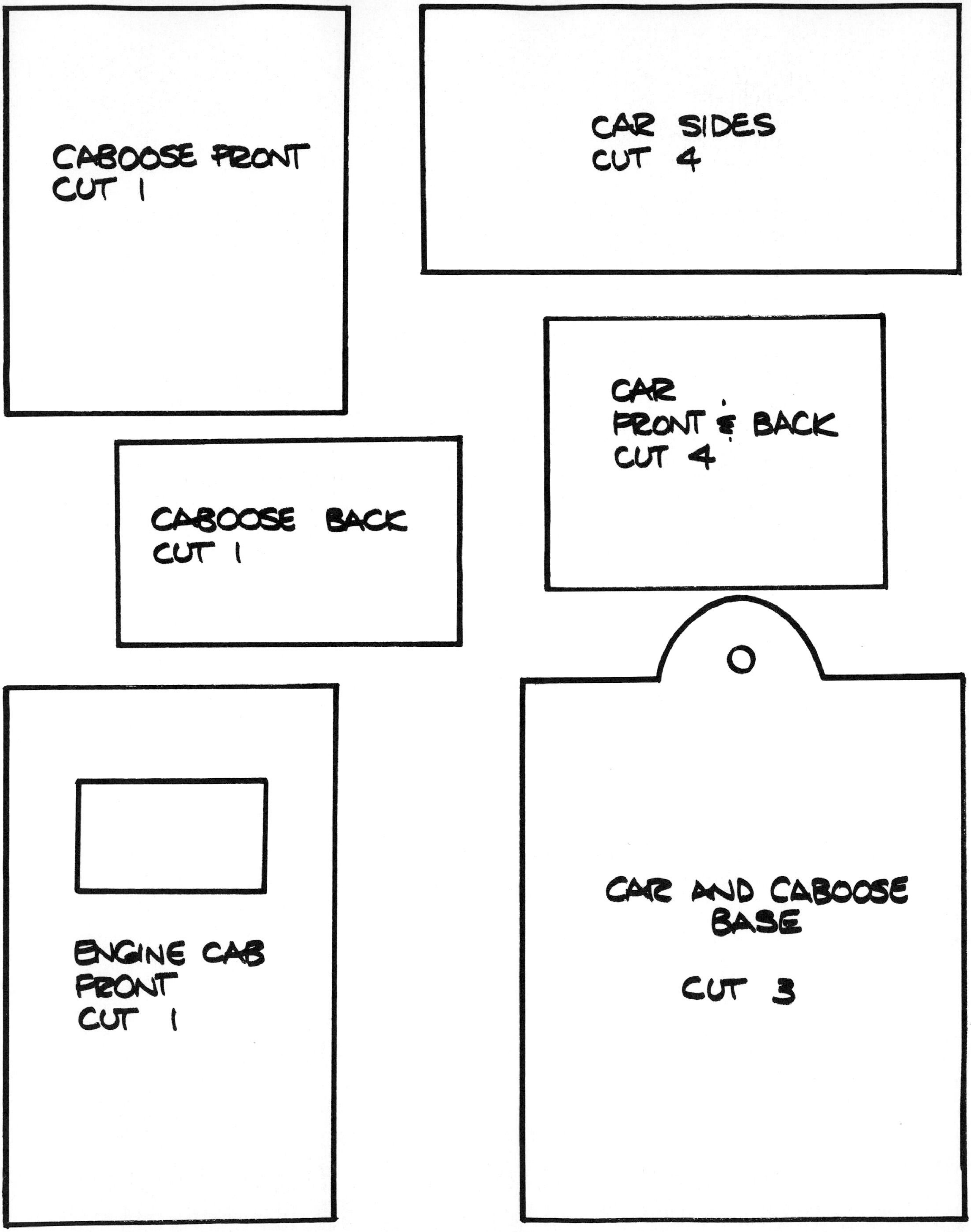

CABOOSE FRONT
CUT 1

CAR SIDES
CUT 4

CABOOSE BACK
CUT 1

CAR
FRONT & BACK
CUT 4

ENGINE CAB
FRONT
CUT 1

CAR AND CABOOSE
BASE

CUT 3

ENGINE CAB SIDES
CUT 2

WINDOW

ENGINE COVER
CUT 1   ROLL 1/8"
WRAP AROUND EMPTY
JUICE CAN

ENGINE CAB BASE
CABOOSE SIDES
CUT 3

CABOOSE AND ENGINE
ROOF   CUT 2

FRONT PLATE
CUT 1

COW CATCHER
CUT 1

97

Icy Swiss Chalet

A small, easy-to-make Swiss chalet is the perfect size for a gift. The tightest space will allow just enough room for this little chalet. The base is foamcore board finished with a narrow ribbon glued to cover the edge. Small cookies may be used in place of candy.

1 batch Architectural
    Dough
1–2 batches Royal Icing
    Hot pink, sky blue,
    yellow and violet
    food color

5 white Drop Flowers
Assorted candy or
    cookies and
    gumdrops
#3 tip
Foamcore base

1. Please read the general directions on pages 10–19. Make cookies and icing.

2. Use a #3 tip and white icing to decorate all sides of house with dots and zigzags. Pipe on window lines. Let dry 20 minutes.

3. Thin icing to flow consistency. Depending on how many chalets you are making, tint appropriate amount of icing hot pink, medium blue, yellow and violet. Fill in shutters and door with hot pink, the panes yellow, the curtains violet and the roof trim blue. Add Drop Flowers and candy. Let dry overnight.

4. Ice edges of sides and press to back. Ice other edge and press on front. Tie string around for support if needed. Ice upper edges and attach roof. Let dry several hours or overnight. Even though this is a small house, it still needs proper drying time.

5. Cover roof with icing. Place gumdrops and a large nougat or caramel for a chimney piece. Place assorted candy or cookies at random. Notice in the picture that there is a variety of shapes, colors, sizes, and texture to the pieces. This variety adds interest.

6. Partially ice base, set house on it and sprinkle lightly with colored sprinkles. Add mint gumdrop bushes at front.

Yield: 1 batch Architectural Dough makes 3 chalets.

BASE IS
6½" x 7½"

ROOF
CUT 2

FRONT AND BACK
CUT 2

SIDES CUT 2

Christmas Tree Centerpiece

This festive Christmas tree will bring color and cheer to your holiday entertaining. The tree, which is easy to make and assemble, provides a backdrop for a variety of decorating options. The miniature ornaments are made of Royal Icing, prepared separately on wax paper and applied once they are dried. You may prefer to use small pieces of candy or simply drape garlands over the tree. The tree rests on a circular base which can be made of gingerbread, cardboard or masonite. Plan for three days of developing time for this project.

1 batch Architectural
  Dough
2–3 batches Royal Icing
  Flow Icing
  Assorted paste food
    colors, especially
    leaf green
  Cinnamon candy
Red Drop Flowers
Approximately 30 red and
  green gumdrops, 15
  each
Approximately 16 tiny
  gift-wrapped boxes
#2, #3, #4, #5 tips

1. Please read the general directions on pages 10–19. Make cookies and icing.

2. You should have one full tree, two tree halves and a base. Trace ornament designs onto a piece of plain paper.

3. Pipe 4 sets of ornaments by slipping tracing paper pattern under a sheet of wax paper. Use a #2 or #3 tip and regular white icing to pipe outlines and important design lines such as clothes, faces and wheels. Repeat three times. Let dry thoroughly.

4. Tint remaining Flow Icing as desired to fill in tiny ornaments, using a #2 or #3 tip. All sections of each little design must touch and be *solid* or it will break, when you remove it from the wax paper. Let ornaments dry 24 hours or longer.

5. Use a #4 tip and white icing to outline base

and one side of tree. All sides will be decorated.

6. Tint one batch of Flow Icing leaf green and fill in tree with a #4 or #5 tip using a back-and-forth motion. How much coverage you will get depends on how thick the icing is and your method of application. If you run out of icing, make more and remember you will need that amount to ice the other side, plus about ¼ cup of regular dark green icing to put tree together. Pull ornaments off the wax paper and place on tree, A helpful hint is to divide ornament designs into two groups. One group always goes on at random on the right hand side of the tree, the other half goes on at random on the left hand side. Do not place ornaments on the center line where the tree will join. Let dry 24 hours.

7. Flip trees over onto soft, clean, dry cloths, such as a towel folded in half. Repeat decorating process for other side and let dry 24 hours.

8. Assemble tree. Generously ice straight edge of tree half with dark green and press to center of whole tree. Repeat for other half. Tie string around tree at each indentation to hold pieces in position while drying. Let dry thoroughly.

9. Make more icing of flow consistency, if needed, to cover base with white icing using a #4 or #5 tip. Place tree in center of base and add gumdrops, alternating red and green around edge.

10. When dry, place tiny "gifts" at base.

Yield: 1 batch Architectural Dough makes 1 tree.

110

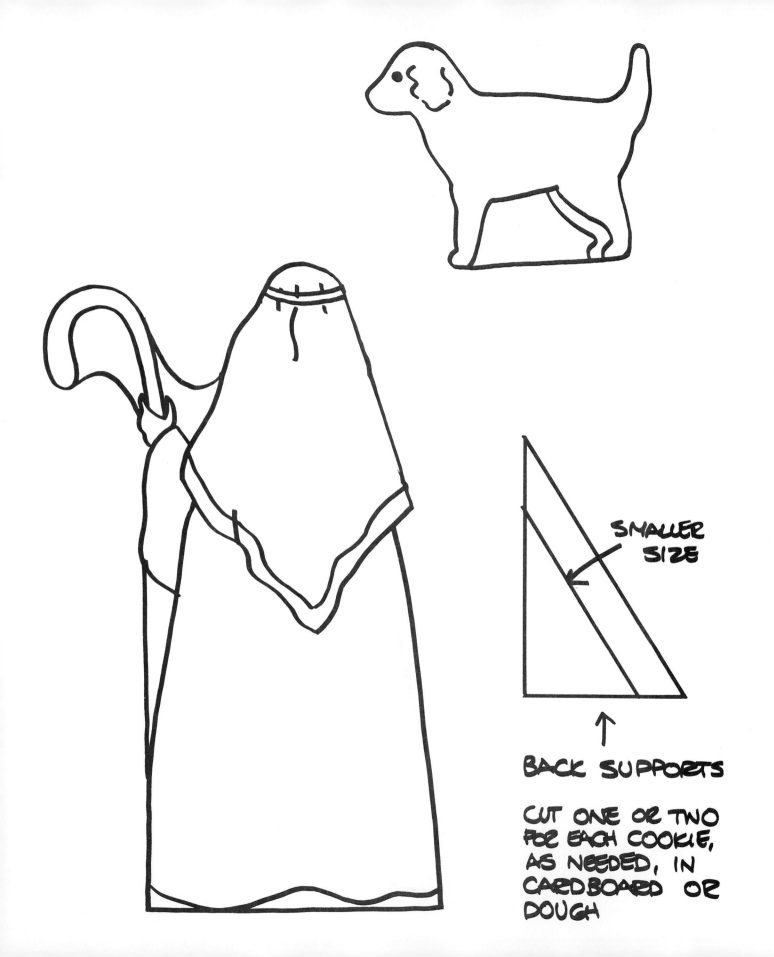

SMALLER
SIZE

BACK SUPPORTS

CUT ONE OR TWO
FOR EACH COOKIE,
AS NEEDED, IN
CARDBOARD OR
DOUGH

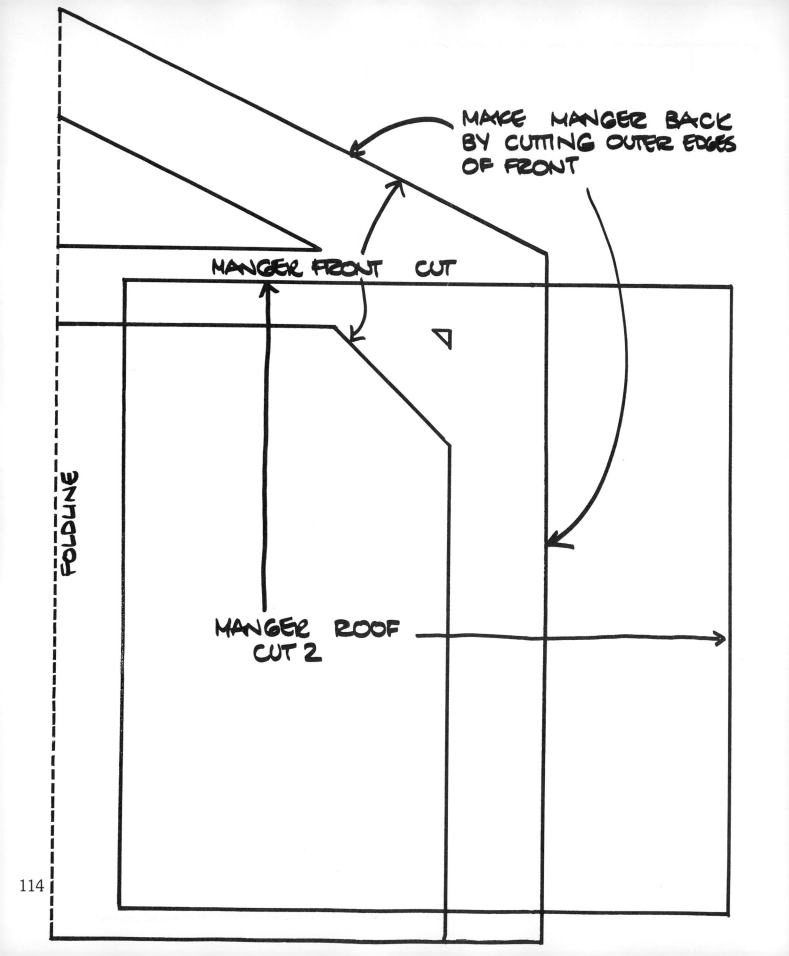

MAKE MANGER BACK
BY CUTTING OUTER EDGES
OF FRONT

MANGER FRONT CUT

FOLDLINE

MANGER ROOF
CUT 2

114

MANGER SIDE

CUT 2

Christmas Tree Ornaments

The use of gingerbread cookies as tree ornaments is a time-honored tradition. Besides adding a decorative flair to the tree, the cookies smell wonderful and, perhaps best of all, can be eaten. (To ensure freshness, wrap the ornaments in cellophane and colored ribbons.)

There are sixteen different designs featured here. The simplicity of each allows for many decorative variations. You may want to decorate just a few designs in various ways to ornament your tree. Or, you may want to achieve the all-out effect of the photograph. Any approach, simple or elaborate, will be a success.

Be sure that the dough is rolled ⅛″ thick to avoid undue heaviness, and provide a hole for hanging.

The ornaments are not just for trees; they may be decorated to place on wreaths, for example, in the old-fashioned style or placed on boughs of holly.

1 batch Architectural Dough
1–2 batches Royal Icing
Flow Icing
Assorted food colors

Drop Flowers
Silver dragees
¼″ red ribbon
#3 tip
Drinking straw, chopsticks, etc. for making holes

1. Please read the general directions on pages 10–19. Make cookies and icing.

2. Be sure to make a hole ½″ from top of cookie with a drinking straw or chopstick before baking. A chopstick will work as well just after baking.

3. Use a #3 tip to fill in major design elements such as outlines, clothes and faces. Let dry 20 minutes.

4. Fill in all white areas first with Flow Icing using a #3 tip. Tint remaining icing as desired and fill in all solid areas with color. Add dragees to drum and soldier's vest. Place Drop Flowers on hearts. Pipe on black edges and add all finishing details.

5. Tie ribbon bows through holes, and add a small metal ornament hanger. Hang on tree for a colorful effect.

Yield: 1 batch Architectural Dough makes 36 ornaments.

119

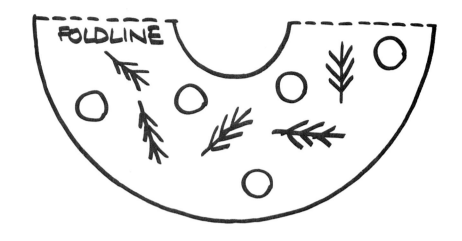

FOLDLINE

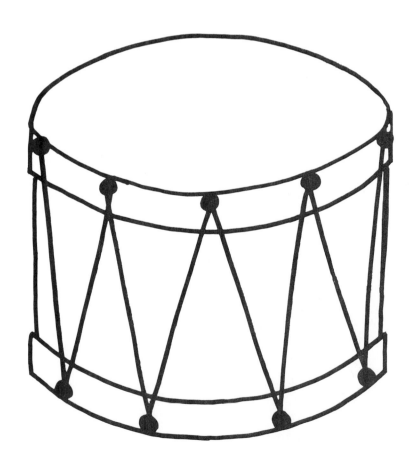

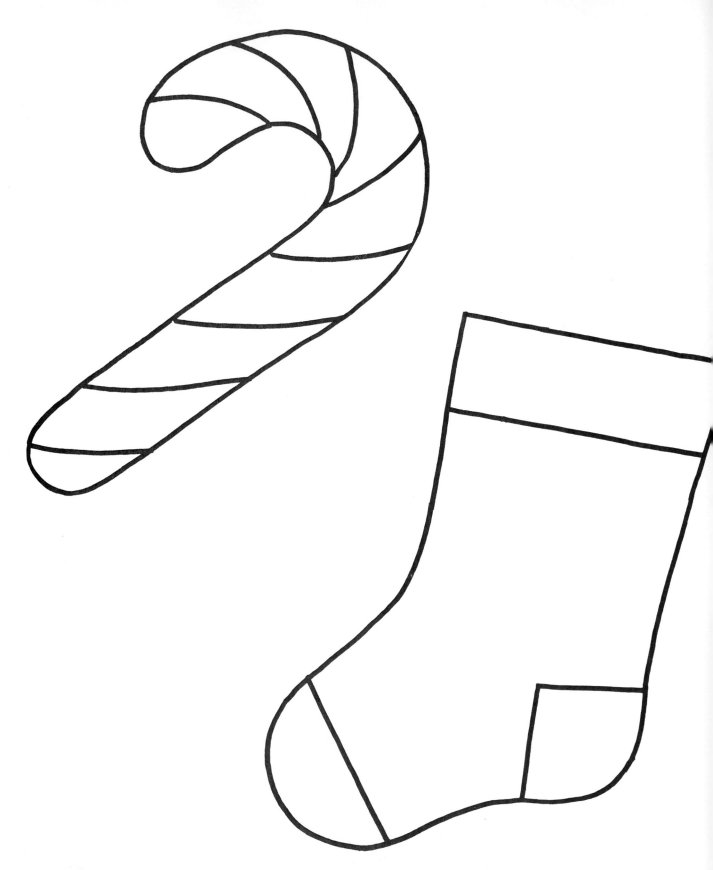

NOEL

Classic House

The quintessential gingerbread project is a house. It is wonderful for a group undertaking, and it's simple enough for children to make, especially if decorated in the manner of the Icy Swiss Chalet. Storebought cookies could be used quickly and attractively for doors and windows. The house design lends itself to many other types of buildings, such as a church. A pattern is given here for a steeple base to use with an ice cream cone steeple. The house can also be lit (directions on page 15). Remember, for best results, allow several days for drying.

1 batch Architectural
    Dough
1–2 batches Royal Icing
    Approximately 50
        small cookies,
        handmade or
        purchased
    Approximately 17
        Drop Flowers
    Approximately 10
        icing hearts

2 small candy canes
4 straight cones
    Hard yellow candy
        (lemon drops) for
        window panes
    Assorted candy
    Green food coloring for
        optional trees
    #3, #14 tip

1. Please read the general directions on pages 10–19. Decide whether your house will be lit. If so, follow detailed instructions on page 15. Make cookies and icing.
2. Cut out all windows and make panes according to instructions on page 22.
3. Decorate walls of cookies. Candy coated gum and a Drop Flower were used for window shutters, pink licorice candy cut to fit with an icing heart formed the window box. Red licorice was used for the door. Cinnamon candy was used at the peak, and a zigzag line was piped with a #3 tip.

131

4. Decorate roof. Arrange cookies on flat roof in four rows of six. Attach with icing. Use candy to fill spaces, and put a dot on top of each cookie. Put chimney together.

5. Decorate and assemble optional trees. Pipe outline using a #3 tip and white icing on whole trees and halves. Fill in with dark green and sprinkle with nonpareils or cinnamon candy. When dry, ice half of the tree edges and press one to each side of the tree.

6. Assemble house. Back windows with yellow candy panes. Support back with jars. Ice side wall edges and press to back wall. Place front of house into position. Support with jars all around. Let dry thoroughly.

7. Ice upper edges of walls and place on roof. Hold in place with jars or cans. Add roof. Let dry thoroughly.

8. Trim straight candy canes to fit at sides and attach with icing. Add peppermint candy to roof-line. Pipe shell edging around roof edge and chimney.

9. Arrange setting with trees and candy.

Yield: 1 batch Architectural Dough makes 1 house and 2–3 trees.

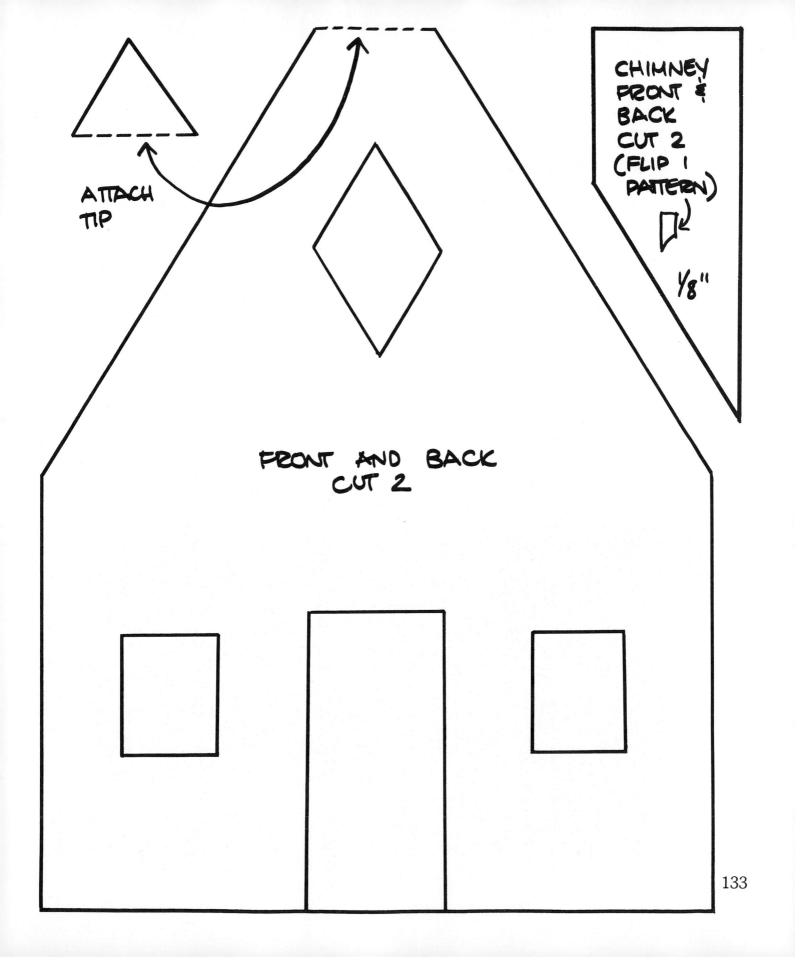

ATTACH TIP

CHIMNEY
FRONT &
BACK
CUT 2
(FLIP 1
PATTERN)

1/8"

FRONT AND BACK
CUT 2

133

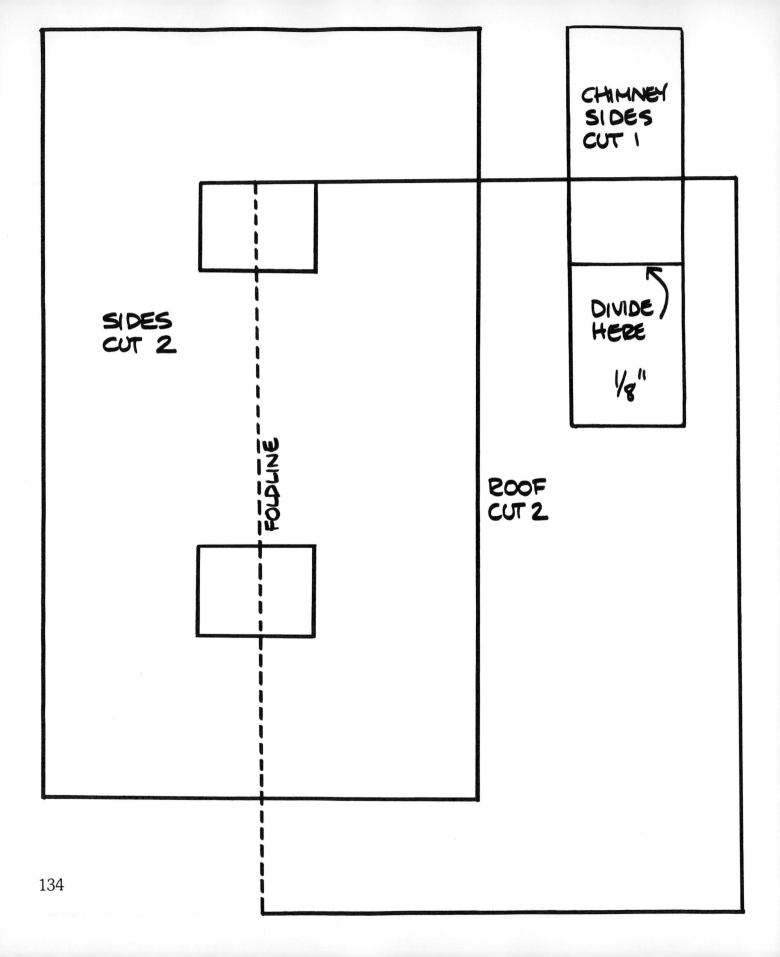

CHIMNEY
SIDES
CUT 1

DIVIDE
HERE

$1/8$"

SIDES
CUT 2

FOLDLINE

ROOF
CUT 2

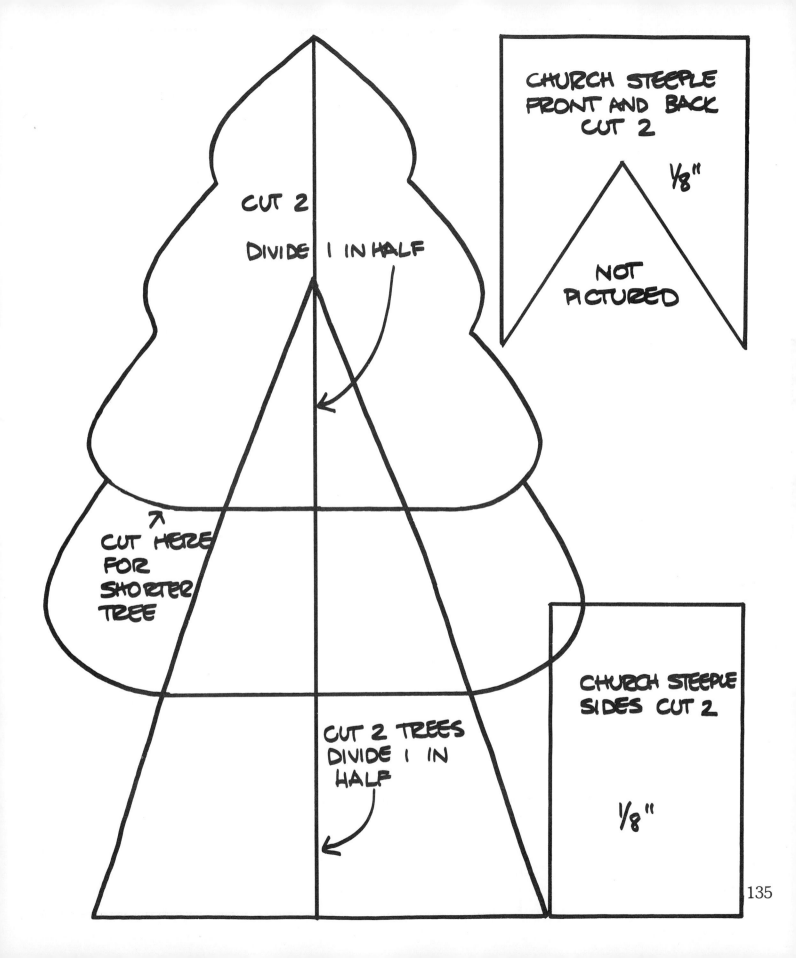

CUT 2

DIVIDE 1 IN HALF

CHURCH STEEPLE
FRONT AND BACK
CUT 2

⅛"

NOT
PICTURED

CUT HERE
FOR
SHORTER
TREE

CHURCH STEEPLE
SIDES CUT 2

⅛"

CUT 2 TREES
DIVIDE 1 IN
HALF

135

Rocking Horse and Gingerbread Boys

Rocking horses have been a beloved American toy since colonial times. This decorative gingerbread version adds a charming touch to table tops and mantels. The basket can be filled with cookies, candy, cards and small lightweight gifts. (Coat basket interior with Royal Icing to prevent grease marks on paper.) Color and trim the horse for festive occasions. By removing the rocker base, you will have a galloping horse. The legs do not have to be cut out. In fact, the piece will be even stronger if the legs are not cut out. Allow two days to make this project, decorate, assemble, and ensure proper drying.

1 batch Architectural Dough*	Flow Icing
1 batch Royal Icing	Silver dragees
	Food colors
	#3 or #4 tip

1. Please read the general directions instructions on pages 10–19. Make cookies and icing.
2. Outline horse, saddle, blanket, eye and feet using desired color and a #3 or #4 tip. The mane will be iced later, over the dry body color, so it does not have to be piped in at this time. Let dry 20 minutes.
3. Tint Flow Icing as desired. For example, leave half the icing white for the Christmas horse. For remaining amount, tint about ¾ red and the rest dark and light green.

4. Use a #3 tip to fill in body areas. Let dry several hours. Fill in remaining areas of solid color and let dry. Pipe on eye, bridle and harness; place silver dragees on line. Let horse dry 12 hours before assembling. If you wish to decorate both sides, flip piece over (when dry, on a soft, clean cloth) and repeat process. Let dry 12 hours; assemble.
5. Place one horse flat on counter, iced side up. Pipe lines where indicated on horse for basket placement. Place bottom piece on first. Ice bot-

tom edges of sides and press firmly in place. Let dry several hours.

6. Ice side edges of basket and stand the horse up. Press both horses together, decorated sides facing same direction, lining up tips. Support horse with hands, applying gentle, steady pressure. It is helpful to place horse in a corner—it lines up tips and supports one horse. Protect horse surface with wax paper. Use a tall, heavy jar or books to hold horse in position. Pipe icing into corners and inside seams as reinforcement.

Pipe top edge of basket decoratively, if you wish.

7. Gingerbread boys have a small zigzag white border, and eyes and mouth made with a #3 tip. Use a #3 tip and slightly thinned red frosting for cheeks and hearts. Don't forget—hearts can be made separately on wax paper, left to dry overnight, then used.

Yield: 1 batch Architectural Dough makes 1 horse and 18 boys.

*Leftover dough can be used for Gingerbread Boys.

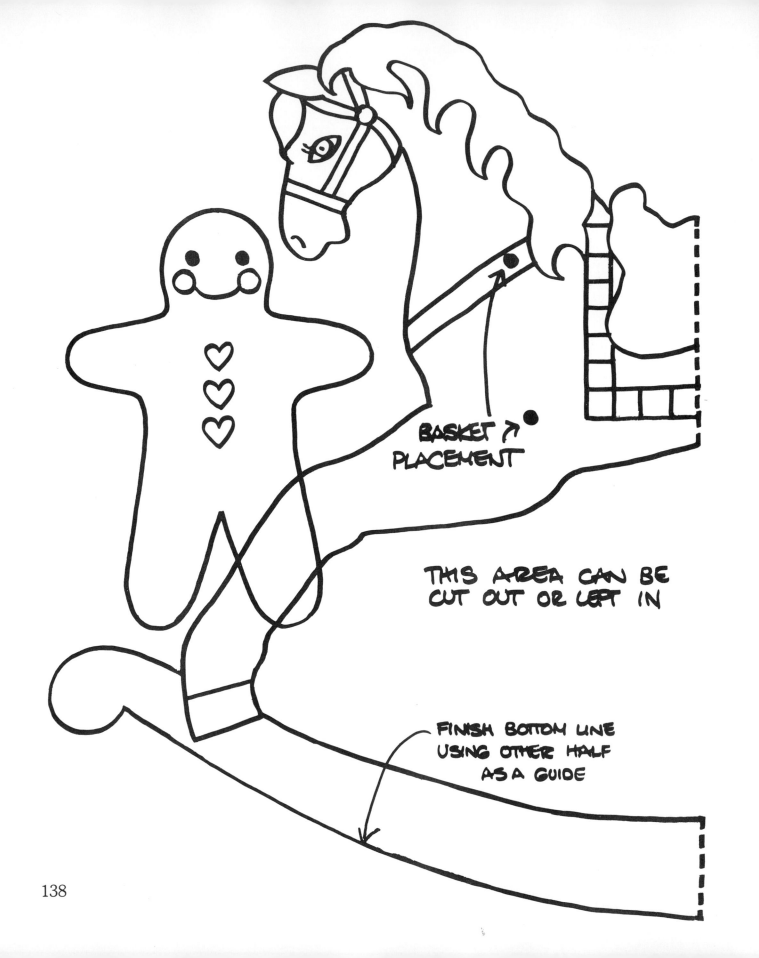

BASKET ⟶ •
PLACEMENT

THIS AREA CAN BE
CUT OUT OR LEFT IN

FINISH BOTTOM LINE
USING OTHER HALF
AS A GUIDE

138

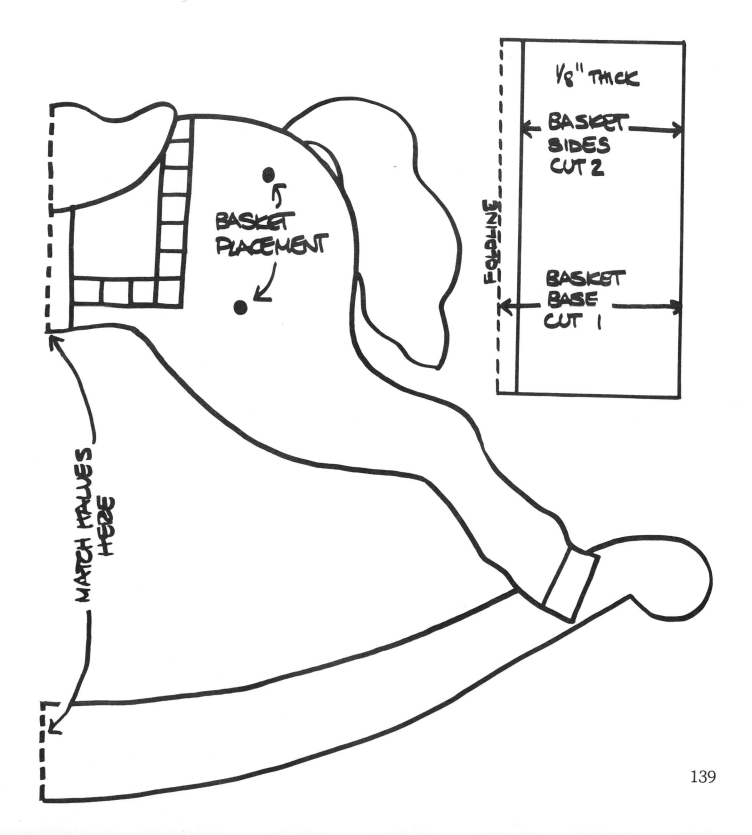

1/8" THICK

BASKET SIDES CUT 2

FOLDLINE

BASKET BASE CUT 1

BASKET PLACEMENT

MATCH MALLIES HERE

INDEX

For information on how you can have **Better Homes and Gardens** delivered to your door, write to: Mr. Robert Austin, P.O. Box 4536, Des Moines, IA 50336.